KI (Chi) . . . *Life Force Energy*
Calligraphy by Masato Nakagawa

Kokoro . . . *Mind / Heart*
Calligraphy by Masahiro Oki

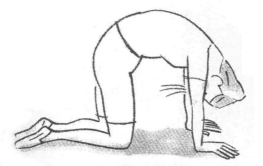

Deep Breath

*Changes Your Body
and Mind / Spirit*

by Osamu Tatsumura

Translation and Foreword by
KAZUKO TATSUMURA HILLYER, PhD

KOKORO PUBLISHING

NEW YORK

Kokoro Publishing
20 West 64th Street, #24E
New York City NY 10023
Tel. No. (212) 799-9711
Fax. No. (212) 799-1661
Email: info@gaiahh.com

The exercises and practices in *Deep Breath Changes Your Body and Mind/Spirit* are not intended to replace the services of your physician or to provide an alternative to profes-sional medical treatment. *Deep Breath Changes Your Body and Mind/Spirit* offers no diagnosis of or treatment for any specific medical problem that you may have. Where it suggests the possible usefulness of certain practices in relation to certain physical problems or mental condition, it does so solely for educational purposes—either to explore the possible relationship of natural breathing to health, or to expose the reader to alternative health and healing approaches.

Printed in the United States

ISBN 978-097049793-2

Designed by Dede Cummings & Daniel Damkoehler
Edited by Ellen Keelan; production by Aleta Alcorn-Coursen
/ *dc*design
Cover art concept by Kazuko Tatsumura Hillyer
The cover design represents the planet earth ("Gaia"), with the top representing blue sky and sunlight, the middle section representing green trees and the brown earth itself, and the red representing the magma beneath the ground.

This edition is printed on recycled, acid-free, paper that meets the American National Standards Institute z39.48 Standard.

Warning – Disclaimer

Acknowledgments

I'd like to give my deepest gratitude and thanks to Yumi Yamaoka, who gave me the opportunity to write this book; Setsuko Kaga, who helped edit it; Mie Kadokuchi, who drew the nice illustrations; Dr. Masaji Nisimoto, whose scientific point of view I consulted; and Atsuko Masuda of Soushi-sha.

Gasshou
Osamu Tatsumura, August 2002

My deepest appreciation to the following people in making this book a reality:

To my spiritual teachers: His Holiness the 14th Dalai Lama of Tibet and Mother Theresa.

To my masters: the late Masahiro Oki and the late Masato Nakagawa, Sr.

To Reimi Takeuchi for assisting me in translating the book.

To Soushisha Co., Ltd and the president Haruo Kitani for their generosity in allowing us publish this translated version in the U.S.

To Mie Kadokuchi, the illustrator, for allowing us to use her original drawings in this English version.

To Dede Cummings and Ellen Keelan for designing and editing the book.

Gasshou
With deepest gratitude, Kazuko Tatsumura OMD, PhD., May 2008

Preface

by Kazuko Tatsumura Hillyer, OMD, Ph.D.

Osamu Tatsumura is my younger brother, and at the same time he is my teacher. Through him, I have learned much of the teaching of the late, legendary Master Masahiro Oki.

After Master Oki's passing, Osamu Tatsumura, as the closest and longest disciple of master Oki, eventually became the leader of Okido Yoga and further developed its unique techniques. Today, he is admired as the most important teacher in the field of holistic healing in Japan, traveling all over the world to teach and give lectures. His book *Deep Breath Changes Your Body and Mind/Sprit* is already a force in Japan, and promises to become a bestseller, helping thousands of people in other parts of the world.

I was taught this unique breathing technique by my great aunt when I was five years old. Then, in 1977, I had a near-fatal car accident and was in the hospital for over three weeks, in a great deal of pain. I will never forget the experience. At the time, my great-aunt came to me in a dream and said, "Kazuko, I taught you. Breathe the way I taught you." I started to breathe, recalling the way I was taught by her. An amazing thing happened: in a few minutes, all my pain and suffering went away! In that hospital I became well known as the "miracle person" who didn't need pain medication! Nowadays, I use this technique in my teaching of the *Onnetsu* method of Far Infra-red heat treatment. My personal experience has made me a strong believer in educating others in it as well.

Breath is life, and to breathe is to live. Correct breathing can do wonders—help you get rid of pain and stress, sleep better, lose weight, quit smoking, and so on and so on. Breathing correctly can help you accomplish more in daily life, and even in business. I'm very happy that this book is now being published in English. I'm sure it will benefit many people throughout the world. Please start using these practices as soon as you can! Thank you.

This book is the third in a series of nine books on health and spirituality being published by KOKORO Publishing. The series includes the following titles:

- *Overcoming Cancer and Other Difficult Diseases in a Holistic Way*, by Tomeko Mitsui and Kazuko Tatsumura Hillyer (published in 2003, second edition in 2007)

- *Your Immune Revolution* and *Healing Your Healing Power*, by Toru Abo & Kazuko Tatsumura Hillyer (published in 2007)

- *Deep Breath Changes Your Body and Mind/Spirit*, by Osamu Tatsumura (published in 2008)

- *Joy of Yoga*, by Masahiro Oki (scheduled for release in 2008)

- *The Mystery of the Body's Relation Points and Okido Corrective Exercises*, by Fernando and Paula Montoto

I hope you will enjoy these books, and please send us comments. Contact Gaia Holistic Health at *www.gaiahh.com* or (212) 799-9711 or *kazuko@gaiahh.com* for more information about upcoming books and how to purchase them.

Contents

Deep Breath Changes Your Body and Mind / Spirit

Chapter 3:
Learning Breathing Techniques

Chapter 4:
EXERCISES 59

For Deeper Breath

Learn Correct Breathing Techniques

EXERCISES, *continued*

Practical Breathing Techniques

Prologue
Breathing Techniques Are
The Wisdom of the East

Every year I travel to Europe and the United States to introduce breathing techniques from Japanese Yoga and the wisdom of the East. Once, when I visited New York several years ago, I was invited to an athletic club. I saw men and women of different ages running on numerous treadmills inside the gym. Many of them were running or walking while reading a newspaper or watching the morning news on a TV on the wall. One person was even running while drinking something for breakfast.

I was convinced that New Yorkers, the busiest people in the U.S., use their exercise time to learn the news or to eat in order to use their time effectively. At the same time, I felt very awkward. They moved their body to burn calories, but their minds and hearts were focused on the news-paper, TV, or drinking. In other words, they exercised with their bodies and minds separated from each other. I know from my own experience that if you keep your body and mind separate, you cannot listen to the voice of your life force, cannot learn from your body, and cannot recognize the connection of body and mind with breath and *Ki* energy. You may solve the problem of getting enough exercise, but you won't gain the wisdom of nature, which can truly help you. You will only use up your energies. These people were actually engaging in wasteful action.

I became greatly concerned when I learned that the same problem is seen in athletic clubs in Japan. People don't know the traditional wisdom of body and mind, including the mechanism of breathing, even though they were born in Japan. This may be because the theories and methods of training that gym trainers and health instructors learn are based on the idea that the body and mind are two different things.

It's quite surprising that the Japanese haven't really recognized how wonderful yoga and breathing techniques are, even though these techniques have been respected as the wisdom of the East by some Westerners who have great awareness. Many know of breathing techniques but don't make use of them. Some don't have the wit to utilize the techniques in their daily life because they learn of them as something outside of ordinary life. If you change your breathing techniques according to need, your stress level, concerns, and physical and mental tiredness will be greatly reduced. You can concentrate or relax when you need to, develop your potential, and act on various aspects of your life without any strain or waste.

I hope that this book will inspire more people to recognize the importance of breathing and help them lead a healthy life with peace of mind.

—*Osamu Tatsumura*

Chapter 1
Deep Breaths and Shallow Breaths

THE IMPORTANCE OF BREATH

At no other time in history have people been as interested in health as they are today. People are seeking not only physical health but also mental stability and peace of mind.

There are many TV shows and magazine articles that report, "This food is effective for _____" or "If you do this exercise you will lose _____ pounds."

But wait a minute. When talking about health, people think of food or exercise right away. Indeed, these things have the power to better our physical and mental condition. But there is something even more important—breath. Breath is the basis and foundation of our physical and mental health, as indicated by the Japanese word *Nagaiki* (longevity), which derives from a word that means long breath.

In yoga, breath is considered the life force. It's said to be a power that eliminates unnecessary and inappropriate matters and toxins, and that refreshes, and that controls metabolism. These concepts are not just from yoga. The word "breath" in English also means life or life force.

In English, breathing capacity is sometimes called vital capacity.

When you look up "vital" in the dictionary, you'll see that it has to do with life or life force. The noun form, "vitality," is used in Japanese as well. Therefore, I hope you now know that breath and life force are deeply related, as shown in these words.

Inhale, exhale, inhale, exhale. . . We keep breathing twenty-four hours a day, awake or asleep, without stop or rest. We breathe literally twenty-four hours a day, seven days a week, from the time we're born until we die.

Do you know how many breaths we take during the course of a life? The number may vary depending on the individual, and increases when you exercise or when you're nervous, but we subconsciously breathe an average of fifteen to eighteen times a minute. It drops to two-thirds or three-quarters of this number at night. So we can estimate that we take about 20,000 to 25,000 breaths a day. If we live for eighty years, we breathe 600 to 700 million times. That's a very large number. Each individual breath may be very subtle, but it has a great influence on our body and mind when we look at the bigger picture.

However, we don't often have the opportunity to be aware of or think about breath in our daily life. Respiratory organs work without our intention because they're controlled by autonomic nerves, like other organs such as the stomach, intestines, liver, and kidneys. We can forget to exercise or eat when we're too busy, but we can't forget to breathe. Respiratory organs will continue breathing. But that doesn't mean we should just let them be. Unlike other internal organs, respiratory organs can be controlled by our will, just like our hands and feet. Learning a better way to breathe—breathing technique, in other words—is the passport to a healthy body and mind.

The way of breathing is not just a technique. It has a deep relationship with your life. Your way of breathing will become your way of living. Even your personality matches your way of breathing. For example, an angry person with a short temper breathes fast. A relaxed and optimistic person doesn't breathe aggressively or weakly. The reason many monks who recite a sutra every day live a long time is that they are trained to take longer breaths without even knowing it.

MODERN MAN'S SHALLOW, SHORT BREATH

For about thirty years, I've instructed people of different sexes, occupations, and ages in breathing techniques through yoga and *Chi Gong*. I have observed that the breathing of Japanese people has definitely become shallow, short, and powerless during these years.

I've also noticed that fewer people manage to keep their backs nice and straight. Both adults and children have bad posture, and obesity is increasing. In 1976, when I first visited the U.S., I was surprised by their obesity problem, which was beyond the Japanese level. However, extremely obese people are becoming less unusual in Japan today.

Obesity is primarily ascribed to diet and lack of exercise, but posture and breathing can be influential as well. (Posture and breathing influence each other, which I'll explain in more detail later in the book.) Breath is controlled by autonomic nerves. When you have bad posture and shallow breathing, it weakens the autonomic nerves, and you'll never feel full when you eat. As a result, you will fall into the trap of overeating and become obese.

But the decline in quality of breathing is not just a superficial problem of posture or obesity. An increasing number of people have less energy or are emotionally unstable. While I can't list every single phenomenon, they prove that the breath of people today is weakening. This problem seems to be weakening our life force, our very power to live. It's not an exaggeration. We may have accomplished an average longer life span, but this is a totally different matter.

Why is shallow breathing bad? It's easier to understand if we think about what good breathing really is. Good, correct breathing is a relaxed long breath: a so-called deep breath. It's a breathing style that sends a lot of air throughout the lungs. It uses the whole body, including the diaphragm, chest muscles, ribs, and collarbone, to breathe.

Shallow breath, on the contrary, is just the opposite. Air is sent to just a small part of the lungs, and the upper and lower parts of the lungs are not used at all. Only the shoulders and chest are used in shallow breathing.

If you made each breath a little deeper, the amount of oxygen that you inhaled per day or even per year would dramatically increase.

The average breathing capacity of a Japanese person in a relaxed state is about 0.4 to 0.5 liters, or 6 to 7.5 liters a minute, assuming there are fifteen breaths per minute. If we simplify this to 7 liters a minute, that would make 420 liters, or 420 milk cartons, per hour, or 10,000 per day. If you increase that amount by 5 percent, 500 more milk cartons of air will be inhaled, which will refresh you.

In reality, however, our quality of breath has been going down. Shallow breath becomes a habit. Today, many people get upset easily, but they don't know that this could be due to their breathing. People often attribute their short temper to stress, but from a different point of view a more serious problem is that their stress is making their breath shallow. But overcoming stress can sometimes make people stronger, happier, and more joyous—so we should not consider stress to be only negative.

MORE AND MORE PEOPLE WHO CANNOT SHUT THEIR MOUTHS!

The Japanese people have another problem with breathing. An increasing number of people cannot breathe well through their nose, and breathe with their mouth instead. I see many people walking on the streets with their mouth open.

Dr. Katsunari Nishihara warns in his book *Kenko Wa Kokyu De Kimaru (Breathing Determines Your Health,* Jitsugyo No Nihon Sha), "This [breathing through the mouth] as a result, weakens our immunity, affects the outbreak of pollen allergy, asthma, nettle rash, and allergies, and creates body constitution that is vulnerable to joint rheumatism or malignant lymphoma. They are all results of abnormality of the immune system." I agree with his theory that breathing through the nose is good and breathing through the mouth is bad.

Traditional yoga breathing methods teach us to breathe in through the nose almost all the time, and sometimes out through the mouth.

When breathing through the nose, dust and various objects and germs in the air are filtered by the nose hair and mucous membranes. When breathing through the mouth, however, objects and germs enter the lungs directly. As a result, you need to maintain a strong immunity against them, which causes your body to strain. If you aren't able to resist the objects and germs, they can cause hay fever, allergic diseases such as asthma, and abnormalities in the immune system.

Of course, there are times when your nose is stuffy and you need to breathe through your mouth. But in general you can reduce strain to your body by breathing through your nose.

Until I read Dr. Nishihara's book, I didn't know that among mammals only humans are structured to be able to breathe through their mouths. We became capable of this when we started walking on our feet. Reptiles and other mammals such as dogs, cats, and monkeys can't breathe through their mouths.

Dogs often stick out their tongues, gasping when it's hot. It may seem that they're breathing through their mouths, but it isn't so. They're actually breathing through their noses and sticking out their tongues with their mouths wide open in order to release heat. The noses of all mammals other than humans are connected to their windpipes, but their mouths can only be temporarily connected at certain times, for instance, when dogs bark.

The human mouth and nose are connected, enabling us to breath through either. However, babies younger than twelve months old can only breathe through their noses. (Though like other mammals, their mouths are connected to their windpipes when they cry.) As they grow, their nostrils separate from their windpipes, enabling them to breathe through their mouths.

Another factor (besides walking upright) that is said to have played a big role in enabling humans to breathe through their mouths is language. Speaking complicated words, rather than simple utterances like a bark, made us capable of breathing through our mouths. It makes sense if you think of babies, who learn to speak as they grow up and start breathing through their mouths.

However, the fact that we can breathe through our mouths is not always positive. The negative aspect is that mouth breathing makes us vulnerable to some immune system problems that damage our physical defense system.

˙ᘐ˙

THE IMPORTANCE OF PARENTAL DISCIPLINE AND SCHOOL EDUCATION

There are an increasing number of people whose breath is shallow and short, who cannot breathe well through their noses and breathe mostly through their mouths. I see adults with this problem, but I see it much more among young children.

Take a few moments to observe how people around you breathe. It may surprise you to see many whose mouths are open. It's obvious that people cannot have clear facial expressions, because their mouths are open loose.

When I was young, our parents and grandparents would warn us when our mouths were open. They would tell us not to chew food with our mouths open, to have a straight back, and to chew well. They disciplined us so that we would breathe through our noses and chew well. When I look back, I see that traditional discipline and manners are not just about appearance, but are actually based on scientific theories and foundations.

How are modern children, on the other hand? They may have fewer opportunities to get such discipline. One reason many children today breathe through their mouths is lack of discipline at home.

Schools don't teach children how to breathe either. What children learn in school about breathing is only partial logic and superficial knowledge. For example, that air consists of $4/5$ nitrogen and $1/5$ oxygen; that oxygen is inhaled and sent to the bloodstream through the lungs, and sent to all the cells in the body through the arteries; that carbon dioxide released from the cells is sent back to the lungs through venous blood. They may learn that plants transform the carbon dioxide released by animals through photosynthesis. They may have a breathing capacity test during physical education class, but only to see if their capacity is more or less than average. Nobody teaches them how to increase their capacity.

A Japanese word, *Iki*, for breath, is phonetically identical to another word, *Iki*, which means to live. Long breath and longevity are deeply related. It's not just a coincidence in Japanese.

Spiritus in Latin and *Anemos* in Greek also mean breath, life, and vitality. There are many things we should learn about breathing in order to live better, but school seems to teach only unimportant matters.

If there were a subject called basic breathing and posture in elementary and middle school a few hours a week, I think the physical and mental health of the Japanese would greatly improve.

When you're nervous or angry, take a long deep breath. Even this simple technique can make things easier. It will help you stay healthy, and you will learn to control yourself naturally. If it's difficult to teach this in school, parents need to teach their children at home.

The Deep Relationship of Chewing and Breathing

Chewing and breathing may not seem to be connected, but there's a very deep relationship. The masticatory muscles that you use when you chew originated from the gills of fish, and they work in relationship with the muscles of the respiratory system. If you chew well, the nerve cells in the brain that affect the respiratory system will be activated, helping to harmonize the respiratory muscles and smooth the mutual relationship that deepens the breath.

Chewing activates the entire brain. One study has shown that old people who chew well are less likely to be forgetful, and those who can't chew well because of poorly made artificial teeth are more likely to be forgetful. Another problem is that children today eat soft food like hamburgers that don't require much chewing, and as a result their breath is becoming shallower. In sum, chewing well when you eat is very important.

Let's take a look at what chewing does. There are three functions:

1. Breaking down and mixing food with saliva to make it easy to digest.
2. Sending information from sensory cells on the tongue and oral cavity to the brain via nerve cells, to activate the automatic secretion of adequate amounts of digestive juices and enzymes for digestion and absorption in the stomach and intestines.
3. Deepening the breath in order to gain a sufficient amount of oxygen for the digestion, absorption, neutralization, and elimination of consumed food.

Therefore, both insufficient chewing and mouth breathing through are factors that make the breath shallow.

THE ENDLESS SPIRAL OF BAD POSTURE
AND BAD BREATHING

Breathing and posture are closely connected. Correct posture is when your back muscles are stretched without tilting to one side and you maintain the natural curvature of the spine. If you breathe correctly and deeply, you naturally have correct posture. I know this from my own experience.

Soon after I began learning yoga, I practiced *Zazen*, sitting meditation in Zen Buddhism. When I was in the sitting position, my back tended to hunch and my chin tended to stick out in front, and every time I fixed my posture it went back to the bad one. I failed no matter how many times I tried, and was disappointed in myself for not being able to maintain good posture. I had no idea why I couldn't.

One day, however, I tried to breathe as deep and long as I could without worrying about posture. I focused on my breath for about half an hour, forgetting about posture, and realized that my posture was remaining correct. At that moment, I became aware that the breath supports the posture. Wrong breathing leads to bad posture. Both influence each other and create a spiral, no matter which one begins it. If you have bad posture, your breath will be shallow and you will tend to breathe through your mouth more, which worsens your posture.

To confirm this, hunch up your back. Your neck naturally sticks out with your head facing upward and your chin sticking out, causing your mouth to be open and your breath to be shallow. On the other hand, if you straighten your back and chest and slightly pull in your chin, you may notice you are breathing more easily and more air is naturally coming in and out.

To improve the bad spiral of posture and breath, you need to begin by correcting your breathing. However, if your posture has been so bad that your body is fixed as it is, it is hard to just correct the breath. You need to correct the distortion of body and *Ki*, which I will discuss later, along with the breath.

In yoga or *Qi Gong*, we treat posture, breath, and mind, or the so-called "Three Secrets," as closely connected.

If you correct your breath, your posture will be correct. If you correct your posture, your breath will be deep. If you correct your breath, your mind will be healthy. If your mind is healthy, your breath will be good.

The key among these three is breathing. If you correct your breathing, your mind becomes more stable and your posture gets better.

I cannot overemphasize that if your posture is bad your breath becomes shallower, and you'll start breathing through your mouth. I've met many old people and have realized that those who have good posture with a straight back and who are not obese tend to be healthy and are less likely to get sick. They're not forgetful, they think like young people, and they are curious and diligent. On the contrary, it seems that if their low back is bent and hunched, they tend to get sick easily and become forgetful at an early age.

To be young and healthy always, you need to learn to breathe correctly.

AIR-CONDITIONING:
THE WORST ENEMY OF "SKIN BREATHING"

Do you know what the respiratory organs are? If you look in a dictionary, it says that the respiratory organs consist of the nostrils, throat, windpipe, bronchus, and lungs. But one other thing can be part of the respiratory system—the skin.

You may have learned about skin breathing in science or biology class. From a biological point of view, skin breathing is the most primitive way of breathing. Earthworms only use this method to breathe. Amphibians like frogs have undeveloped lungs, which they supplement by breathing through their skin.

What about humans? According to modern science, the amount of air that we take in through the skin is less than 1 percent that of the lungs. But I personally feel it's more than that.

I was an actor in college. One time I had to dance with white greasepaint all over my body. Normally, I could dance for thirty minutes without feeling tired, but I couldn't last more than ten minutes, probably because my pores were blocked with paint.

Skin has a very important role in addition to breathing—controlling body heat. Skin opens and closes the sweat glands to release or maintain heat to control body temperature.

Until a few decades ago, it was normal to sweat when it was hot in the summer, and for our skin to tighten in the cold. That was natural. Look at how things are today. Buildings, trains, cars, and houses are air-conditioned. The temperature is artificially set to about 20°C (68°F) throughout the year, and we no longer sweat much. Our ability to breathe through our skin becomes weaker when we spend all our time in air-conditioned rooms, because there are fewer natural opportunities for the skin to expand and shrink. We become disconnected from the natural environment, unable to feel the different seasons with our body, and when we're not exposed to seasonal changes our immunity becomes weaker. This is a problem.

Skin eliminates, too. We eliminate unnecessary waste matter in our body not only as stool and urine, but also as sweat. If you don't have enough opportunities to sweat, you end up storing the waste. When the waste that's supposed to be released by sweating builds up in our body, we become more vulnerable to catching a cold. Have you noticed that it feels like your pores are clogged before you get sick? If you go to a sauna to sweat, you may be able to avoid getting sick. If you and your skin feel clear, your physical and emotional elimination systems are working well.

The functions of the skin are more important than we think. When it's hot, we should sweat. It's good to go to a sauna regularly or jog in order to sweat. It is also important to find opportunities for your skin to stretch.

Animals in the wild naturally increase their body fat to prepare for the cold winter. Their fur becomes longer and warmer to adapt to cold weather, and falls off in the spring. This kind of adaptation occurs naturally within the body to follow changes in the weather. But we humans have created an artificial environment in which we no longer need to adapt to nature. As a result, we're more likely to get sick. Air-conditioning is one of modern society's problems.

Even if you know how harmful air-conditioning is to your skin and body, you may have no choice but to work in an air-conditioned environment.

The pores in the skin expand when it's hot and shrink when it's cold. But as this stretching ability becomes weaker, we become less able to adapt to changing weather, and become less immune to the cold.

When the skin is not able to open or close the pores well, we can't eliminate *Jaki*, or negative energy, very well. That negative energy builds up, making us more vulnerable to disease. That's what we believe in Eastern medicine.

If you think you have this problem, try the following bathing methods: First, alternate bathing in warm water and showering with cold water repeatedly. If you have two tubs, use one for cold water and another for hot water, bathing in the two tubs consecutively and repeating the process several times. If bathing in cold water is too difficult, start with lukewarm water until you get used to it. One trick is to breathe out on the sound "haaaaa" as you get into the cold water.

As you become accustomed to this bathing method, you'll begin to breathe through your skin more, and your body will become so healthy that you won't get sick easily. You may feel energetic and clean when you're naked. This clean feeling is the sign of an active flow of energy due to active skin breathing.

The second way to activate your skin is to rub you body with a towel. The traditional wisdom of a mother rubbing her weak child with a towel and a prayer seems to have been forgotten.

Rub your body with a dry towel until your skin is slightly red.

BREATH IS IMPORTANT IN JOGGING, WALKING, AND CHILDBIRTH

Jogging and walking are very popular. It may be a sign that people are beginning to pay attention to their health.

There's so much information based on numbers, such as "Run with this much pulse per minute" or "You burn this many calories if you walk this many kilometers" or "You'll lose this much weight in this many days if you run this much every day." There's also talk about form, such as "Your pace should be this much," "Your arms should swing like this as you walk," or "You should keep your arms at this angle, and your legs. . ." Unfortunately, though, people almost never talk about breathing.

From my own experience, I know that I feel less tired when I move in harmony with the rhythm of my breath. Moving in accord with the breath makes exercise more effective too.

We think of jogging and walking as physical exercises in which you move your body, but they'll be more effective if you practice them as breathing exercises. If you run in accord with the rhythm "inhale, inhale, exhale, exhale" or "inhale, exhale, exhale, exhale," the strain on your body will be dramatically reduced and you'll notice the difference in how you feel (see p.141).

You'll become more aware of and sensitive to your condition, so you can stop exercising or continue to exercise based on how you feel.

Breathing also plays an important role is the delivery of a baby. While this is something I can never experience myself, I have had the opportunity to teach maternity yoga at the request of an obstetrician.

This doctor encouraged his patients to practice the Lamaze method for natural childbirth. However, even though they practiced several times in preparation, they often failed to follow the doctor's guidance at the time of delivery.

I instructed these women in breathing methods to accompany certain movements, called maternity yoga. The result was unexpectedly successful. I instructed women who were at least five months pregnant and had never practiced yoga, and they learned to strain and relax their bodies at their will using breath and movement. Some even told me that the breathing techniques enabled them to find balance and gain a better understanding of their body's condition.

Breathing techniques using only the respiratory muscles weren't effective for these women. However, once they learned to breathe in combination with movement, like yoga, the practice was much more effective. It is very interesting that they were able to control their breath, contractions, and the loosening of their muscles when they breathed with movement.

LACK OF OXYGEN CAUSES MANY DISEASES

If your breath is shallow, the quality of your blood will be low. This means that the blood has less oxygen, instead of being thick and having a lot of cholesterol, as is frequently discussed today. Hemoglobin in the blood absorbs and sends out oxygen to the cells all over the body, but when oxygen is lacking, blood won't flow. The oxygen absorbed by the hemoglobin is low. Or, in medical terms, we say the saturation of oxygen is low.

Cells can't work efficiently without oxygen and will die in the end. If you continue shallow breathing, your cells can't rejuvenate due to lack of oxygen, the elimination of waste matter doesn't take place, and therefore the internal organs can't function well. It's also said that cells lacking oxygen can sometimes cause variants like cancer.

Another problem is diet. Our society today is all about satiation. We always eat until we're full. However, we need only a little amount in order to survive, so most of the food we eat is not absorbed and becomes waste. Or it's stored in our body as fat.

The power that transforms food into nutrition is breath. If you eat too much and lack oxygen, you can't burn nutrition into energy sufficiently. It becomes pure waste.

Shallow breathing is one of the factors that make modern people unhealthy. We need to realize this problem. But what causes shallow breathing? Let's take a good look at some causes.

1. Autonomic nerve imbalance, caused by stress
2. Stiffness of the muscles around the respiratory system
3. Distortion of the spine
4. Lowering of the positions of organs such as the stomach and ribs
5. Swelling of the internal organs
6. Constipation
7. Problems of the respiratory system

I've already discussed the relationship between posture and breath. You may be surprised at number 5, swelling of the internal organs, or number 6, constipation. Swelling of the internal organs may include swelling of the liver. In Eastern medicine and yoga, there are techniques whereby one can read an abnormality of the liver without looking at medical test results. Here's one easy example: Lie on your back and gently push the area along the bottom of the right rib with your fingers. If it's painful, your liver is exhausted. According to my experience, many people who have a short temper, overeat, eat fast food frequently, or are in administrative jobs with a lot of stress are likely to have this problem. If your liver is swollen or if you have constipation, your stomach area is always tense and your breathing tends to be shallow.

Learn to breathe deeply and slowly with the correct technique. If your blood has more oxygen, your cells will be more active.

You can control your breath to a certain point with your intention, but it's also controlled by your subconscious, because it's so closely related to life itself. In other words, it's controlled by the autonomic nerves. If you have deep, relaxed, and stable breath, your autonomic nerves will be stable as well. This will result in a high secretion of hormones. Autonomic nerves consist of sympathetic and parasympathetic nerves, and both will function smoothly in balance, increasing your immune power and natural healing ability. Your brain will work better and your mind will be fflexible and generous.

Learn to breathe deeply and slowly with long, deep, rhythmical breaths for a body and mind in good condition.

꘎

Can Oxygen Be Toxic? What Is Active Oxygen?

We cannot live without oxygen, but did you know that oxygen can damage us?

You may know that the surface of a piece of cut apple gets brown or that iron rusts because of oxygen. Or that if you block oxygen by wrapping food in plastic, you can avoid the oxidation of food—in other words, the degradation of protein or fat.

Actually, the body uses this oxidation system to defend itself against bacteria, viruses, and foreign objects. The organism has a system for attacking and destroying foreign objects that enter the body by creating highly active oxygen from inhaled oxygen. White cells kill bacteria by activating the oxygen they take in, using it to sterilize and protect the body while they eat the bacteria. If this active oxygen were produced as much as needed, whenever needed, there would be no problem.

But today we have more opportunities to get nervous and excited from exhaust gas, cigarette smoke, food chemicals, and additives taken into the body, as well as by stress. This causes us to produce excessive amounts of active oxygen in the body, which in turn damages the body itself.

Active oxygen plays a big role in cancer, diabetes, arteriosclerosis, and other lifestyle-related diseases. However, it is now known that an appropriate diet and a stable mind can prevent the production of active oxygen. For example, polyphenol in green tea and vitamins C and E function as antioxidants in the body, preventing our body from oxidizing. That's why antioxidant food and health products are gaining a lot of attention now.

Chapter 2
Breath and Ki

SEIZA, YOGA, AND BREATHING TECHNIQUES

I first became interested in breathing techniques when my mother told me this story. My mother was born near the end of the Meiji period and was a practitioner of *Seiza*, Japanese silent sitting meditation, in the Okada Method. This sitting method was started by Torajiro Okada (1872–1920) as a physical and mental training, breathing technique, and meditation technique, and was very popular from the end of the Meiji period until the mid-Taisho period. His analects were dictated by his students, and many are still around today: "Just sit in silence." "When you sit in silence, you will be aware." "Your heart is the original. The nature is the translation of your heart. Books are the translation of nature. They are the translation of translation." "When you practice *Seiza*, you develop your wisdom, virtue, body, and all. When you improve your mind and body by training, you can unfold your innate ability." "Acknowledge the transcendent great art in your every single breath." And so on. He was an educator who emphasized the importance of the breathing method that focuses on *Tanden*.

My grandfather on my mother's side, Sazou Kojima, was a medical doctor in Tennoji, Osaka. Unfortunately, I only know him from my mother's stories because he died before I was born. My grandfather studied a primitive version of what is now called psychosomatic medicine and lectured once a week at what is today the medical school of Kanazawa University. I also heard that he was a follower of the Pure Land sect of Buddhism, and that he treated the poor who couldn't pay for free.

There is no doubt that my mother, inffuenced by her father, studied the Okada Method. My aunt, who was adopted by Dr. Sansaburo Kobayashi and his wife, Nobuko, of Seizasha in Kyoto, succeeded them in the Okada Method. Because of this, my mother joined the gathering held at the Kobayashi's once a month.

I went to gatherings with my mother, but they weren't interesting to me, especially as an elementary school student. I didn't understand why I had to sit for such a long time.

When I was in middle school, my mother told me a story whose details I don't recall. In essence, she told me that she had delivered nine children, but that only eight survived, and that she had also miscarried another baby. It was a very cold day, she was doing a physical labor, and a sharp pain stung her stomach area. It was too late to do anything, and she miscarried. She told me that she went into a panic because there was nobody around to help her. What came into her mind when she was trying to think of what to do was *Seiza*. She sat with a correct posture and endured using the Okada breathing method.

She said, "There was nothing I could do about the miscarriage, but thanks to *Seiza*, it didn't cause any further problems."

As a result, ever since I was a small child, I had a vague idea that breathing and correct posture are very important, but I didn't have the opportunity to study any further.

In the spring of 1971, I started practicing yoga as part of my theater training. I think it was about half a year later that I came to experience something unforgettable.

Back then, nobody in the theater club, myself included, understood yoga very well. In fact, now I understand that even the instructor of the theater company who was teaching us yoga did not have a profound knowledge of yoga, even though he had been to a yoga dojo. We practiced various things, including holding the breath with our eyes closed, without really understanding what yoga was all about.

I thought it was a good thing to be able to hold my breath for a long time because I'd heard that holding your breath was very important in yoga. So I kept practicing holding my breath as long as I could (*Kumbaku Method*), then exhaling when I couldn't hold it anymore, then inhaling and holding my breath again for a long time. It gives me a cold sweat now to think about it. But we were serious about it back then.

One day, after holding my breath several times, I suddenly fainted. I was in a sitting position on the wooden ffoor and I fell forward, hitting my forehead on the ffoor. Thanks to the pain, I became conscious, but I didn't know what had happened to me. But the next moment, I felt a strong sensation of fear that I had never felt before. I experienced a near death. That experience was so vivid that I wrote about it in a literary coterie magazine that my friends and I published.

After graduating from college, I went to a training facility for physical trainers of adults. I intended to become certified as a yoga instructor. I was hesitant because of financial problems when I was in school, but I decided to join a seminar at Oki Yoga Dojo with money that I borrowed. This was at the end of 1973. Here, I met Master Masahiro Oki, who changed my life forever. I was overwhelmed by his *Ki* impact, *Ki* power, and his energy.

That's how I came to learn yoga and breathing techniques.

I also had another unforgettable experience, when I was working as a physical trainer at a training room in a gym in Tokyo about twice a week.

Few people came to use the training room in the morning, so I sat down on a mat with warm, spring-like sunlight on my back, in order to practice the "*a-o-m*" breathing method. For this breathing meditation, you practice with your voice about ten times, and then repeat the sound within your heart.

I was very focused on repeating this method for about twenty or thirty minutes. I had practiced this many times before, but I had a unique experience that day. I felt as if I were embraced by a golden light, and at the same time I felt a bliss that I had never before experienced.

I wished it would last forever, but my wish was soon destroyed by the sound of a person entering the room. The bliss that I was feeling also went away.

Around the same time, I read an article about a Westerner who had a mystical experience of *Samadhi* during meditation in India, and I thought his experience might have been similar to mine. But no matter how much I tried doing the same thing, I could never experience that bliss again.

When I shared my experience with Master Oki later, he told me that the important thing is not to be caught up in such an experience. He also told me that the truth of yoga is not something special, something apart from mundane life. After that I stopped thinking about the meaning of the experience or seeking it again.

When you practice breathing techniques, you may have such an experience of bliss. Please note that this is a temporary experience and that it is neither essential nor important.

BREATHING TECHNIQUES WERE INSPIRED BY ANIMALS

I often travel to India to get in touch with the roots of yoga and breathing techniques. There, I had an opportunity to listen to an interesting story about *Prana* from Dr. Nathmal Tatia, the president of Jainism University and the Nalanda Buddhist Monastery. It's a story from the Upanishad, a classic, esoteric text of their religious philosophy.

The brothers of the "Life" family—"Breath," "Mouth (word)," "Eyes," "Ears," and "Thought"—one day discussed who was the greatest among them. They could not come to a conclusion. So they asked their father, who said, "The greatest one is the one who would make the body suffer the most if he were absent." So Mouth left the body and came back a year later. He asked, "Were you in trouble without me?" and they answered, "We couldn't speak, but we could breathe with Breath, see with Eyes, hear with Ears, and think with Thought for a year." There was some inconvenience, but they could survive by supporting and complementing each other. Eyes, Ears, and Thought also left, but the body could survive with the functions that were left without much difficulty. At last, when Breath was about to leave, everyone else realized how problematic it would be, and said "Please don't go. Breath is the greatest among us."

In this classic Indian story, breath is regarded as the most important of all functions, the foundation for all others.

In India, there is a story that's been passed down: All living things of the same type breathe the same number of times in a lifetime. Those who breathe short breaths many times a day live a short life. On the other hand, those who breathe long breaths fewer times live a long life. They observed wild animals thoroughly and realized that turtles, snakes, and cranes, for example, breathe long breaths.

There are also breathing techniques in India and China that imitate animals, such as "bear's breath," "monkey's breath," and "deer's breath."

A person who practices yoga is called a yogi, and yogis in the past have created many breathing techniques inspired by animals. I suspect that by imitating animals' breathing, they were trying to regain the natural wild power within humans, which had long been lost.

Here, I'd like to introduce cat's pose for breathing (see below). One of the typical poses inspired by animals, this is a very easy pose that anyone can do. It is particularly effective for easing back pain in pregnant women, but is recommended for anyone who would like to relax. It may feel good to stretch muscles that you rarely stretch in your daily life.

What ancient people sought in breath was not the inhaling and exhaling of air or techniques such as thoracic or abdominal respiration. I think imitating the way animals are and how they breathe was the origin of the practice of breathing techniques.

By imitating animals, we can refresh our mind and body, releasing the flow of *Ki* or the pattern of breath, which is suppressed in human society.

INSEPARABLE BREATH, *KI*, AND MIND

Breath is a very profound matter, with many aspects and functions. Looking just at the physical aspects, breath is about taking in oxygen and releasing carbon dioxide, or how much breathing capacity there is.

But another function of the breath is to control the flow of *Ki*, although this cannot be scientifically proven at this time.

Let's discuss *Ki* in more detail. When your stomach is not well, if you stimulate certain acupuncture points with an acupuncture needle or fingers such as the hollow point below the kneecap outside the shin, you will feel soon better. Or if you have a toothache or stiff shoulder, you can

Cat's Pose

1. Inhale first, and as you exhale arch your back, with your head between your arms.

2. Come back to the center as you inhale. Then, stretch your spine down, dropping the navel and face looking up, as you exhale.

3. Come back to center as you inhale.

ease the pain by stimulating a point between the thumb and index finger. This kind of knowledge is very common in Japan.

In a traditional Eastern viewpoint, it is said that there is an invisible flow of *Ki* throughout the body that is spread the same way that a fishnet, blood vessels, or nerves are spread. It's also said that *Ki* goes in and out through acupuncture points. When your energy is stagnant, causing pain, you can stimulate acupuncture points on the line related to the area of pain in order to move the stagnant *Ki* and balance the flow of energy throughout the body, easing the pain.

We can't see the flow of *Ki* or acupuncture points, even if we dissect a human body. But we cannot deny that there's a flow of energy, because you can definitely improve unhealthy areas of your body by stimulating acupuncture points.

In the type of yoga and *Qi Gong* that I have studied, we believe that our visible physical body is a vessel that holds *Ki*, or energy, which allows us to live. In other words, this energy vitalizes our life. Every moment, our *Ki* is transforming as it flows in and out throughout our body, never stagnant.

Let's take a look at our body and *Ki* from the point of view of breathing. You can't breathe deeply if your body is inflexible, your shoulder is stiff, or if the solar plexus isn't stretched. If you do certain physical exercises to stretch the muscles in the chest in order to loosen the cartilage of the ribs so they can be flexible, you can breathe deeply. This is breathing at the physical level. The more you inhale, the more oxygen gets into your system. I'm sure you can all understand this.

Now, what about breathing at the *Ki* level? You may find it a little complicated. If you don't move your *Ki*, you can't breathe more deeply. Even if you try to breathe deeply, you can't achieve much if you focus only on the physical level. That's why we need to practice breathing techniques in order to move *Ki*. These techniques not only help you take air in and out, they also help move *Ki*. There are also different conditions of *Ki*, such as whether its quality is good or bad, whether or not it's flowing well and how much, and whether or not it's distributed in a good balance. These qualities influence us physically and mentally.

Breathing techniques that move *Ki* influence us to move our consciousness or mind at the same time. Moving our consciousness is not visible either, but the effect that air has on our body and mind can be completely different depending on whether you think the air smells bad or whether you think the air is fresh and feels good. Different results come if you work hard, with your mind focused, rather than superficially. That's how we move *Ki* and our consciousness or mind with breath.

Physically deep and relaxed breath can lead to a stable and self-controlled mind. If you observe how your mind changes very carefully, you can see how it's related to changes in your breath. When you're relaxed, your breath is slow and calm, but when you're stressed out, your breath is short and shallow.

Therefore, it's important to remember that our body, *Ki*, and mind are correlated, and influence each other. This is very important in my method, which I introduce in this book. I call it the Tatsumura Breathing Method.

THE ESCAPING FROM WOLVES BY LAUGHING METHOD

I'd like to emphasize how important breathing practices by sharing a story that Master Oki told me.

A long time ago, Master Oki was meditating under a tree in a deep mountain in India. One night he suddenly realized that he was surrounded by numerous shining objects. When he looked carefully, he realized that these objects were the eyes of a dozen or more wolves shining in the dark.

The wolves were observing him closely and cautiously, waiting for a chance to attack him. Even Master Oki was overwhelmed by fear, but he managed to calm himself by consciously breathing very deeply to slowly strengthen his abdomen (*Tanden*). Staying alert the whole time, he thought of what he should do. There was nothing nearby to protect him or to use as a weapon.

He observed the wolves as he thought about how to escape, and he realized that there was an important pattern in their movements. The wolves were taking a step toward him as he breathed in, and pausing and watching him as he exhaled. That meant that when he breathed in, he was off guard, giving them a chance to attack, and when he breathed out, they were more cautious.

Master Oki remembered the "laughter method," which he had learned with his senior masters. This is a breathing technique in which you laugh hard and loud, with exaggeration when exhale. He started to laugh with force and a loud voice: "Ha ha ha ha ha ha…" It actually scared the wolves, and they ran away.

Master Oki quickly climbed up the tree while they were gone. The wolves came back soon. They stared at him in the tree, but it was too late. They hung around under the tree until dawn, but once the sun was up they gave up and went away.

Whatever the situation may be, it's important to breathe slowly in order to lower the *Ki* in your body and calm yourself. I learned from this story that, when you breathe out slowly, it's possible to come up with ideas to help you handle a situation and act appropriately.

APPLYING CELESTIAL *KI*

The world view we subconsciously have today is very different from when yoga and *Qi Gong* were developed. I believe we can easily overlook the essential meaning of breathing or movement instruction if we view them with modern ways of thinking.

For example, if someone asks why we should eat carrots, we may say, "Carrots have beta-carotene and are anti-carcinogens. They're also rich in fiber and. . ." We say, "You should eat a lot of carrots because they're good for you." When we choose what to eat, we focus on the material-istic aspects of food, such as the chemicals in them and their nutritional factors. I've heard that, at supermarkets and grocery stores, perfectly shaped vegetables, whether a carrot or a radish, sell before distorted ones. This too is a very superficial, materialistic way of choosing.

Did people in the past choose the way we do? What would they focus on in picking one carrot over another? They didn't know about carotenes. I'm sure they picked something that looked nice and fresh, like we do. I personally think they also picked something very powerful and lively, even if it was distorted. In other words, they chose the one in which they could feel the presence of "energy." There are carrots that seem stronger and those that seem weaker. Carrots are alive too.

I think we are no longer able to see the *Ki,* or energy, in food because we consider food a material object and are so focused on judging it by the way it looks. Because of this, we have less appreciation than people in the past had for food, for receiving the life of a carrot with gratitude as you eat it.

In yoga, *Ki* is called *Prana.* About the time I began learning yoga, I asked Master Oki a question. "Master, is *Prana* oxygen?" I was surprised by his unexpected answer, which was "*Prana* is an energy that allows everything to live." That struck me. I had never thought of it that way. It opened my eyes to the idea that there is a force that allows us to live as we do. If my master had explained to me, "*Prana* is not oxygen. It is an unidentified object that hasn't been proven by science," I might have been satisfied by the answer, although it would have still been a mystery. But I had never heard of or studied a philosophy that focused on the fact that we live, that there is an internal power that allows us to live and an external force that allows us to live. I realized that subconsciously I had a materialistic world view and that I was attached to scientific explanation, and I have since tried to be more cautious of my point of view and my mind.

In the type of yoga that I learned from Master Oki, *Ki* can be separated into three major categories: celestial *Ki,* human *Ki,* and earthly *Ki.* This yoga teaches us to take in celestial *Ki* through breathing techniques, human *Ki* through learning, and earthly *Ki* through food, in order to utilize and apply them.

I didn't understand then why breathing, eating, and learning were taught in the same genre of *Prana Yama,* or the control and application of *Ki.* I thought that breathing in and out, and consuming nutrition such as protein and calories were totally separate matters. Moreover, I wondered why learning by reading books or listening to lectures was taught as a study in the same manner as breathing

However, as I continued to study yoga and breathing techniques more profoundly, I came to realize that my way of understanding was biased. We have to look at these three different kinds of *Ki* from the viewpoint of "an internal power that allows us to live and an external force that allows us to live."

For example, imagine that someone in front of you suddenly stops breathing. Their pulse will soon be gone as well. Something that was going in and out when they were alive is no longer there, and the pulse that was sending it through the body stops too. They will be lifeless and won't respond if you call their name. I've had the experience of closely watching someone die. When celestial *Ki* stops flowing in, it means death.

If you don't eat, it's obvious that you will slowly die of hunger. Those who can't eat lose weight and power, and die eventually. Food gives us earthly *Ki*.

Both celestial *Ki* and earthly *Ki* are the source of the force that allows us to be alive. Look at the sky and the earth again, with this thought. You will realize that there should be a breathing method that seeks to bring in force from heaven and apply it. You'll also understand the importance of an eating method that studies how to better utilize the food we receive from the earth.

And finally, human *Ki*. Humans are born into the human world and grow into humans among other humans. In Japanese, 人間, meaning humans, literally means "being among humans." There are things that are passed down from parents to children. We can be strong and lively or lose enthusiasm, depending on our environment, education, or the influence of other people. That is human *Ki*, and that's how we learn.

When you realize that you are allowed to be alive, it is important to utilize the force that allows you to live without wasting it.

GETTING ANGRY, UPSET, AND MAD

Almost every day lately, many bloody, horrifying events take place. Recently, someone was beaten to death by a person who got upset when he was asked to move farther for other people on a crowded train. Even young children have committed cruel murders. They overreact abnormally to things that are very insignificant to normal people. Many people today have these dramatic reactions, though not always to the point that they murder other people.

We need to think about why this is happening. It's true that various kinds of stress are increasing in our society. But that's not a good excuse for such abnormal behavior.

I think it's because the *Ki* of modern man is usually very unbalanced and concentrated toward the head and upper body. In other words, *Ki* is not flowing to the stomach area.

In Japanese, we say when we were angry, "My stomach is standing up." What do we say today? We use terms such as "I'm feeling sick in the chest" or "I snap" when we're angry. It's in our chest area that gets the sick feeling, and our head that snaps. This shows how the center of energy has moved from the stomach to the chest and then to the head. I don't know exactly when we started using the term "snap," but it must have been in the last several years. It must be in the last ten years or so that "feeling sick in the chest" began being used to indicate anger.

In the past, we were disciplined by our parents and schools to focus our *Ki*, or energy, in the abdomen. People in the past used the word *Jokyokajitsu* (upper body empty and relaxed, lower body in full force), to indicate that our upper body is empty and that all the strength is actually in the lower body, which is our natural state of being. We often say "Let's be natural," but that only means relax the body. Even if we think we're relaxed, our body may be stiff. *Jokyokajitsu* is a condition in which the upper body is totally relaxed and all the force is in our stomach or lower back. This is the natural way of being.

School systems before the World Wars were manipulated by militarism, but they had some good points as well. This is off the topic, but there was a class called *Shushin* (mastering body) where we were taught ethics and discipline. But after the wars, the wrong idea prevailed that religion can't be involved in education. I think we need to distinguish religious groups and personal religious beliefs. It is absolutely necessary to have faith as long as we are human. It's important to teach not to kill and to respect other lives. That doesn't mean we have to belong to a specific religious group or sect. We no longer even teach such basic principles in our daily life or in the school system.

Going back to my point, the school system today does not teach children to settle *Ki* in their stomachs. Education is focused simply on knowledge.

There's no longer education about the stomach. As a result, *Ki* has continued to move upward all the way to the head. This energy is now settled in the head because the *Ki* is entirely imbalanced, preventing good ffow.

I'd like you to learn how to breathe by lowering the center of *Ki* to your stomach. Even if your energy is in the upper part of your body, you still inhale air by breathing. It may not be sufficient because you breathe shallow and short with your mouth, but there is still air coming in and out. However, you may not succeed in controlling *Ki* with your breath.

If you master this breathing method, and succeed in lowering your *Ki*, your breathing capacity will be bigger. But that's not the only advantage. You will become naturally focused on your stomach. You will be able to think and judge with your stomach. If your *Ki*, or energy, is centered around your stomach or lower back, you will be a very stable person who won't easily get mad or upset.

PRACTICAL BREATHING METHODS FOR DAILY LIFE

You may think that breathing techniques are something for which you always have to follow rules and steps. But that's for an introductory level of breathing techniques, not real breathing techniques. The real idea of breathing techniques is that you can apply methods that are appropriate and necessary for each situation. Doing so should put you into a balanced state of body and mind that will enable you to do things the right way.

I always emphasize that it's more important to regard different postures and actions in our daily life as breathing techniques, rather than to work on breathing techniques as just an isolated practice. Of course, beginners will need to follow the instructions as they practice certain breathing methods. But over time, you will deepen your understanding of breath and *Ki* as you apply the techniques and *Ki* to different life circumstances, and you will learn to control yourself well without being limited by the practice. This will help you to be stronger and you won't get tired as much, you'll learn thing more quickly, and so on.

There have been many breathing methods passed down to us for centuries. Their purpose is to give you a foundation so that you can breathe right according to the situation.

In Oki Yoga, the type of yoga I have studied, there is a training method called *Tanden* Strengthening Breathing Method, which is a good example of a live breathing technique training that can be applied to every situation. As part of this training, we crawl on our hands and knees like a crocodile or a primitive kind of frog, or we move like a shrimp jumping. We imitate the movements of animals. When you breathe during such movements, you can create unusual *Ki* flow throughout your body, which activates nerves and muscles related to the respiratory system, transforming your breath itself.

We also had the following training: In our dojo of 80 tatami mats, there were stages a few feet tall, from which Master Oki told us to jump like a cat without making any noise. His students jumped off one by one, starting with the seniors. Master Oki gave them instructions particular to each student, such as to breathe out, tighten their anus, or jump off laughing.

Everyone was afraid at the beginning and couldn't jump well, but as they repeated the exercise with Master's instructions, they were able to jump off almost without making any noise. As for me, I couldn't do it well at the beginning, and sometimes I felt pain in my feet when I jumped off. However, I started to understand how to do it well, and I became good to the point that I was always appointed by Master to demonstrate.

The trick to doing this well without making noise is breath. Jump off as you breathe out forcefully, releasing and moving the impact of landing up through the legs, knees, and hips. It is actually the control of the breath that determines whether your muscles are tense when you land or whether you're able to receive the impact softly like a cat and control your force to ease the impact.

In this book, I'm not going to introduce techniques for special occasions, like jumping off a high wall. Rather, I'd like to introduce breathing techniques that can be applied to our daily lives—breathing methods to lead your posture or make your movements more efficient. The fastest way to master these is to practice them with movement.

Overcoming Fear with
the Tight Anal Breathing Method

The following happened while I was learning how to strengthen *Tanden* at the Oki Yoga training dojo when I was in my twenties.

Master Oki gathered us, his students, outside, and told us that he wanted to do some strength training outdoors at a new training facility. The training facility, which we had never used before, was like a tower about twenty feet tall, constructed of H-shaped steel, each piece about eight inches wide.

Master told me to climb up and walk on top of it. Since I was good at such training exercises as walking on the balance beam, I began climbing the tower without hesitation. I had no problem until I was on top of it looking down. I was surprised by the height, which was more than I had expected, and I couldn't take my hands off of the steel. It was as if they were frozen.

I heard my master yelling, "What are you doing? Walk now!" I wanted to walk, but my hands wouldn't let go of the steel.

I took several deep breaths with my butt hole tightened, remembering my master's words to tighten the anus and take deep breaths in the event of trouble. Then I gained control of my hands, and they let go of the steel. Luckily, I was able to walk to the other side of the eight-inch-wide steel in front of the other students.

It was the first time I had experienced my conscious and subconscious fighting face to face.

It was also an experience in which I learned that I could calm myself down by breathing deeply and tightening my anus.

Chapter 3
Learning Breathing Techniques

THE BASIS OF BREATHING IS EXHALING

Before we get to actual practice, let me talk about the basics of breathing and breathing methods.

One technique that most Japanese learn first is deep breath. This is a technique that we always do at the end of our radio exercise in the morning. You may have taken deep breaths at the beginning and end of physical education classes, after you work on joints such as your wrists and ankles. If so, I suspect that you always followed the pattern "breathe in deeply and breathe out."

A Japanese word for breath is written 呼吸, or *Kokyu*. Exhaling (呼) comes before inhaling (吸). Try to breathe in after you breathe out with a "ha" sound. You should be able to breathe more air deeply. Our ancestors must have known that we need to exhale before inhaling.

In an old Shinto practice in Japan, we call breathing techniques *ibuki*, or breath, and we focus on exhaling. That's because we believe that we can purify ourselves by breathing out, so that we can receive the divine *Ki*, or breath of God, in. Our *Ki* will be unclean if the flow of *Ki* is blocked, so we exhale first.

Center your breath on the exhale. Please keep this in mind, because it is a very important principle and the basis for all breathing techniques.

Exhaling and inhaling is the rhythm of contraction and expansion, traditionally called the rhythm of yin and yang—the fundamental power of the universe, centripetal force and centrifugal force, manifested in the organisms. The greater the difference between "inhaling" and "exhaling," the greater the amount of the air that will come in and out, and the fuller one's life force will be.

If you practice exhaling completely, the respiratory muscles such as the diaphragm and abdominal muscles will contract, making it automatically easier for the chest and stomach to expand and breathe more. You can train your respiratory muscles efficiently by focusing on exhaling because you use more muscles with less force when you breathe out than when you breathe in.

THE DIFFERENCE BETWEEN THORACIC BREATHING AND ABDOMINAL BREATHING

It was about when I started learning yoga that one of the senior students told me that I should practice abdominal breathing because it was important. I hadn't studied any breathing techniques in yoga, so I didn't really know what thoracic and abdominal breathing were. I had a vague idea that thoracic breathing was bad and that abdominal breathing was good. Later, I was told that *Tanden* breathing was the best technique, and that abdominal breathing was not enough.

As I continued to study breathing techniques, I came to realize that most people fail to do both thoracic and abdominal breathing. When I observed the breath of someone who had studied at a Zen dojo for twenty years, I noticed that he was good at abdominal breathing and that his stomach expanded and contracted very well. But he told me that he had often had back pain or a stiff shoulder. I also noticed that someone who had practiced *Tanden* breathing for years still had very inflexible shoulder joints and a hard time stretching their arms. I realized that people who benefit from breathing techniques for the purpose of recovering their health tend not to pursue the study further after a certain point.

Tanden breathing is an application of abdominal breathing that brings *Ki* to *Tanden*. Therefore, I found it a pity that some people con-

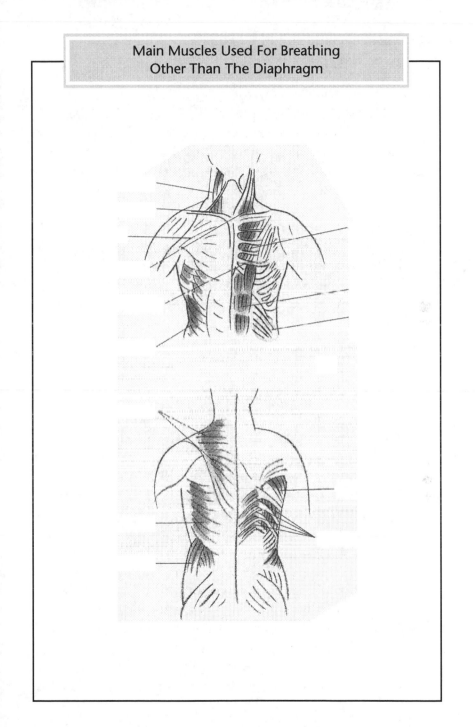

sider *Tanden* breathing a totally different technique and do not practice the basics of abdominal breathing.

Abdominal Breathing Technique

Abdominal breathing technique gets its name from the fact that it looks as if the air enters the stomach as you breathe, making it move back and forth. However, it is actually the diaphragm that moves up and down, changing the internal and external pressure of the lungs and letting the air come in and out.

Thoracic Breathing Technique

This technique allows the air to come in and out according to the movement of the ribs, which change the pressure.

We normally breathe with a mixture of abdominal and thoracic breathing. However, most people fail to breathe perfectly, and therefore their breath tends to be shallow. People with stiff shoulders, neck, or solar plexus; humpbacks; those who cannot fold their hands on their backs or whose arms are stiff cannot possibly deepen their breath. It is more important that they increase the flexibility of the muscles that affect the breath, and reduce mental or emotional stress by learning how to relax.

In the yoga tradition, we train to expand the muscles of the chest and stomach to create a foundation for deep breath by practicing yoga asana, a physical exercise that is completed prior to breathing techniques. My breathing capacity was about 3700 CC before I started doing yoga, but it increased by 1500 CC afterwards. I am only 164 cm, and not big at all, but I was able to increase my lung capacity to 5200 CC.

As I discussed previously, we unconsciously breathe about fifteen to eighteen times a minute in a normal state, but it is said that we use only 10 to 16 percent of our maximum breathing capacity. It's no exaggeration to say that you can change all aspects of your life by using the highest capacity of your lungs, even for only a few minutes a day.

But why is abdominal breathing considered to be better than thoracic breathing?

Abdominal breathing enforces the movement of the diaphragm, which massages the internal organs; therefore, it improves blood circula-

Expansion and Contraction of the Rib Cage, Lungs, and Diaphragm in Breathing

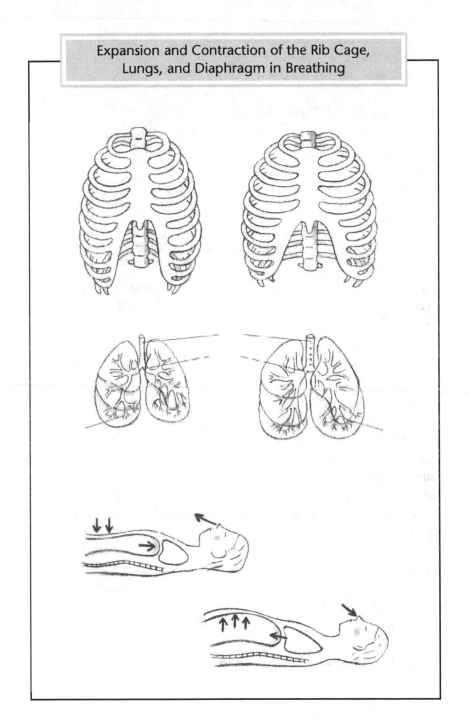

tion and the functions of the internal organs. It eliminates congestion in the lower organs, which is caused by our lifestyle of standing on two legs, and improves bad blood circulation in the organs.

I'll discuss *Tanden* breathing later, but you can consider it one of the abdominal breathing techniques.

If you practice breathing out with force, contracting the diaphragm and abdominal muscles, your chest and abdomen will automatically expand easily so you can breathe in more air.

Before you say, "I have to do this technique, or that technique," it's important that you breathe out strongly.

THE IMPORTANCE OF BLOOD IN CONNECTING EXTERNAL AND INTERNAL BREATH

When we speak of breathing, we usually mean the exchange of oxygen and carbon dioxide that takes place between the lungs and the outer world. This is called "external breathing."

Oxygen in the air that we breathe is taken into the blood and sent out to the cells of different systems through arteries. There, the exchange of oxygen and carbon dioxide takes place at the cellular level. This is called "internal breathing."

Living organisms need to take in nutritional substances from the outer world and transform them into energy in order to live. Oxygen is required to burn these substances into energy. Carbon dioxide is eliminated as an unnecessary substance during this process. This inner breathing of cells is more fundamental for organisms than external breathing. All living things, including fish and earthworms, conduct inner breathing.

Of course, external breathing plays an important role. Imperfect external breath makes internal breath imperfect as well. Cells working with insufficient oxygen cause imperfect combustion and elimination. This weakens the cells and hastens their aging process.

Cells lacking oxygen can eventually cause diseases such as cancer. Three major causes of death today are cancer, cerebrovascular accident, and heart disease, all of which may be caused by a lack of oxygen in the blood, which as a result prevents internal breathing.

Blood vessel problem in the brain mean an interruption of the distribution of oxygen to the brain cells. Coronary artery problems in the heart area shut out the distribution of oxygen to the heart cells. Even if the other parts of the body are healthy, this can lead to a fatal problem.

For internal breathing to be successful, sufficient external breath is necessary. But is it enough? For correct internal breathing, the blood needs to carry a sufficient amount of oxygen. If you are anemic or have bad blood circulation, your internal breath won't be sufficient even if your breathing capacity is high. In other words, the quality, amount, and circulation of blood are key.

Food and mind are the greatest influences on the blood. In modern medicine, it is thought that blood is produced in the bone marrow—but does that mean that food is just for energy and calories? No, it doesn't. Traditionally, we say "food becomes our blood and flesh." Absorption of food by the intestines is very important to the absorption of ingredients for blood.

I think a meat eating diet is not appropriate for the Japanese body constitution because it causes the blood to be slimy, which may block the blood vessels. The diet most suitable for the Japanese includes grains as a main dish and a vegetarian protein such as fermented soy or tofu as a side dish. This kind of traditional diet does not create much trouble in the process of digestion, absorption, neutralization, and elimination.

One way to determine the quality of your blood is to see whether you have resistance to disease when people around you have a cold, or whether you recover relatively quickly from a wound or disease. Blood that suits you is good blood that can maintain high immune power.

But having good blood suitable to you and mastering deep breath by practicing breathing techniques isn't enough. For successful internal breathing, you need to have good blood circulation. For this, you need to exercise. However, exercise can sometimes cause an imbalance or damage the body, depending on how you exercise, so you need to be careful.

Running improves blood circulation in the major muscles and the heart but can sometimes strain the body too much. In addition, it doesn't necessarily improve *Ki* flow or blood circulation to the smaller muscles and other organs.

Therefore, I recommend that you walk rather than run. One reason is that it is relatively easy for anyone to do. Also, as we say, "legs are the second heart"; contraction and expansion of the muscles in the back of the legs allows the blood to return. In other words, walking can improve the flowing back of the blood.

One recent big problem is Economy Class Syndrome. This happens when you sit in a small seat on an airplane for a long time and your blood doesn't circulate back to the heart very well. Veins deep inside the femurs get clogged and cause phlebothrombosis. When you are on an airplane where you cannot walk around, you should occasionally stretch your Achilles tendons, calves, and the insteps of your feet.

Needless to say, it is important that you always walk at a speed and time appropriate for your condition. The way you walk is also very important. If you have pain in your knees or back when you walk, you should correct the distortion of your body first.

Even if you manage to master all of this, it is still insufficient when it comes to improving the blood circulation and *Ki* flow of the organs. Therefore, I'd like to recommend some yoga postures. Yoga is not necessarily a sport. In yoga, you continue to breathe deeply and focus your mind while keeping complicated postures and movements. Therefore, it is really a breathing exercise.

Yoga is done this way because it causes the stagnant *Ki* and congested blood to flow and truly improves blood circulation.

In normal exercise, *Ki* moves in the muscle group that is being actively used, but not in muscles that are contracted and useless. When you practice yoga postures, on the other hand, the muscle stiffness and contraction that prevent good breathing are eliminated, and you can breathe more deeply.

LAUGHTER AS EXPIRATION, CRY AS INHALATION

Scientifically, breathing is "taking in oxygen and releasing carbon dioxide."

At ground level, air is composed of 79.02% nitrogen, 20.94% oxygen, and 0.04% carbon dioxide. This is the air we inhale. But it comes out of our body with a different constitution: 79.02% nitrogen, 16.30%

oxygen, and 4.50% carbon dioxide. In other words, what we expire is still three-quarters oxygen.

Artificial respiration for a drowning person is usually done mouth to mouth. This shows us that the constitution of expired air is sufficient to revive someone. This is the case because the respiratory nerves are stimulated and awakened more by the practitioner's *Ki* and by the contraction and expansion of the respiratory system than by the oxygen in the air.

Respiratory movement not only carries oxygen to the cells, it also influences our body and mind in various ways. For example, when it functions as a flow of *Ki*, expiration tenses and stimulates the muscles. Inhalation, on the other hand, relaxes the muscles. Think about bending forward to stretch, for example. If you exhale as you bend forward, you will be better at bending than if you were inhaling. When you fall while practicing martial arts or exercising, you're less likely to get injured if you breathe out and more likely to if you breathe in. This principle can be applied to many occurrences in daily life, so I recommend that you keep this in mind.

If you want to excite or energize yourself by using breath, breathe in with your chest wide open, which stimulates the sympathetic nerves, and beat your chest like a gorilla. If you exhale longer and more slowly than you inhale, it stimulates the parasympathetic nerves and you will naturally calm down.

When you get injured and feel pain, rather than stopping the breath, screaming "ouch! ouch! ouch!" you should consciously breathe out very strongly with a "haaaa" sound, and continue exhaling with a groan. (This is called the groaning breathing technique.) You will feel less pain, and the pain will be gone sooner. This also prevents the contracted muscles from causing more problems later.

When you breathe in, your center of gravity, or *Ki*, moves up, and when you breathe out, it moves down. You can apply this consciously. For example, in a judo match it is easier to attack the opponent when they're breathing in or about to breathe in, and if you breathe out when they attack you, you will be less vulnerable. When you breathe in, you can be unguarded.

If your energy rises to your head and your mind goes blank when you're about to give a speech, you can bring the energy down and calm yourself faster by exhaling and doing Shiko (a type of exercise used by Sumo wrestlers at the beginning of match, in which they raise their legs one at a time and stamp the ground, lowering their body position and bringing down *Ki*).

When you cry, your inhalation is more exaggerated. When you laugh, your exhalation is naturally more exaggerated. Even if there's nothing to laugh about, if you go "ha ha ha," you can bring out a feeling of laughter from deep within your emotions.

In breathing techniques, there is inhalation, exhalation, and holding. There are two methods of holding your breath: one for after you inhale, and one for after you exhale. When we want to encourage ourselves after aturally breathe in and hold the breath quietly. When you hold your breath after inhaling, you can concentrate or focus your power into an important point. This is called Kumbak in yoga, and it is very important because it awakens vital force. You don't hold Kumbak in your chest. You exhale about half of what you inhaled and bring the rest down to your stomach. Your lower belly expands and you tighten your anus. Traditional yoga teaches you to inhale for one count, hold for four counts, and exhale for two counts. If you breathe in this proportion, you can improve your biological and mental activities to their highest capacity.

Affects of inhalation and exhalation to one's body

	Muscles	Autonomic Nerves	Senses	Focus of Weight	Autonomic Nerves	Emotional expression
Inhalation	Tensed	Sympathetic	Excited	Up	Excited	Cry
Exhalation	Relaxed	Parasympa-thetic	Calm	Down	Calm	Laugh

BRING OUT YOUR BREATHING CAPACITY
WITH A PERFECT BREATHING TECHNIQUE

In yoga, we categorize the types of imperfect breathing that people normally do into three categories. When we perfect all of these and combine them, we'll have a "perfect breathing technique" or "total breathing technique." We also teach that we need to train in order to master this perfect breathing and achieve spiritual enlightenment.

I have discussed earlier there are so-called "thoracic respiration" and "abdominal respiration," More accurately, there are three different kinds of imperfect breathing, as noted below. Most people habitually use one of them to breathe.

IMPERFECT BREATHING

ffi U𝔪𝔪 𝔪𝔪 𝔪𝔪𝔪 This is the worst of all three types. It's also called collarbone breathing because the shoulders, collarbone, and upper chest move up and down when one breathes this way. There's rarely any movement in the stomach, abdomen, diaphragm, or ribs.

Among the three types of imperfect breathing, upper lung breathing allows the least amount of air to enter the lungs. Therefore it's not efficient, despite the amount of energy needed to move the muscles of the chest, shoulders, and neck. If you're accustomed to this type of breathing, your jaw sticks out forward, your shoulders are raised, and you're humpbacked. Many people with chronic stomach problems, respiratory problems, or neuroses tend to have this habitual way of breathing.

ffi M𝔪𝔪𝔪𝔪 This is also called rib breathing because it moves the ribs. In this way of breathing, partial contraction and expansion of the rib cage forces the air in and out, but the diaphragm tends to move upward. There's not much up-and-down movement and the abdominal cavity is retracted and doesn't move much. This is more efficient than upper lung breathing, but less efficient than lower lung breathing. Since it moves the chest, people often call this "thoracic breathing."

This type of breathing tends to be done by people who don't know breathing techniques; who have stiff shoulders, neck, and back; or who can't relax.

ffi L𝔪𝔪 𝔪𝔪 𝔪𝔪𝔪 This is also called diaphragm breathing because the diaphragm's up-and-down movement pumps air in and out of the lungs. The diaphragm is shaped like a dome at the time of exhalation, and moves down at inhalation, putting pressure on the organs in the abdominal cavity and pushing them forward. This is what's called "abdominal breathing."

Lower lung breathing takes air into the lower and middle parts of the lungs but doesn't fill them up to the top. In this respect, it's not perfect, but it's far better and more efficient than the two previous kinds. When you're on your hands and knees like dog and cat, you naturally breathe this way. This is what most humans have forgotten to do now as we stand upright to live.

If someone who habitually uses the first two breathing styles can master lower lung breathing, his breath will be remarkably deep and his physical and mental health will improve. In fact, practicing lower lung breathing, or diaphragm or abdominal breathing, has been considered very important for a long time, and has become synonymous with breathing technique for health.

The Tanden breathing method lowers the diaphragm as you exhale, putting pressure on the stomach to focus *Ki* into the Tanden. It can be considered a type of diaphragm breathing because it moves the diaphragm up and down.

PERFECT BREATHING (TOTAL BREATHING)

The purpose of the perfect breathing technique in yoga is not just to inhale and exhale air, but to activate our innate physical and mental ability to breathe. It is the foundation by which to control and use *Ki*, or Prana—the power to keep us alive.

How should we move the muscles that surround the respiratory system in order to move the diaphragm up and down and expand and contract the ribs front and back, right to left, and up and down, in order to breathe? We need to observe this, study it consciously, and practice step by step so that the air spreads all over the upper, middle, and lower parts. This type of breathing is also called total breathing because it makes the best use of the lungs, ribs, diaphragm, and muscles of the respiratory system.

Total breathing requires you to consciously expand the lower, middle, and upper parts successively. Of course, nobody can do it perfectly at the beginning. In addition, if you don't enhance the flexibility of the respiratory system muscles or the joints of the thoracic bones and ribs, you may think that the amount you can expand and contract right now is your limit.

There are three steps in total breathing: inhaling, holding, and exhaling. Hold your breath after you breathe in, as I described earlier. Hold for a few seconds to begin with. As you keep practicing, you'll manage to hold longer without putting pressure on the lungs. If you continue to practice, you will begin to notice the correlation of mind and breath, of the consistency of oxygen in the blood and the way you feel, and of the air and *Ki*, or Prana. This is the basis of bringing *Ki* to your body and mind.

I explain how to do total breathing on p.93.

BREATHING TECHNIQUE IS MORE EFFECTIVE THAN EXTREME ASCETICISM FOR BUDDHA- LIKE ENLIGHTENMENT

Many people throughout history have included breathing techniques as part of their spiritual training. The oldest and most famous of all of these people, as recorded in existing literature, is Shakyamuni Buddha. I wonder what Buddha thought of breathing. We can make some assumptions based on what's been told of Buddha's life story.

It is said that Buddha primarily practiced meditation and extreme ascetism between age 29, when he decided to take on the spiritual path, and age 35, when he reached enlightenment.

He studied with Alara Kalama, a holy sage, who taught him dhamma which led him to the realm of Nothingness." He also studied with a sage, Udaka or Ramaputta, where he was able to realize the stage of Neither Perception nor Non-perception, but he left them, believing that none of them would lead him to the Nirvana that he was seeking.

Buddha then went to Uruvela Forest where he practiced extreme austerities with other fellow seekers of enlightenment, which were believed to lead one to liberation," These kinds of extreme ascetic trainings are called *Tapas*, which means heat. The meaning behind this term is that one needs to have a strong mind that won't be damaged by exposing the body to burning heat, in order to release the spirit from the entanglement of the physical body.

Some training methods back then were accompanied by pain and straining. Buddha disciplined himself by meditating under the burning sun, being naked in cold weather, fasting, holding his breath, and so on. He totally devoted himself to this training for six years, as no one else could have done.

But he noted this result: "The harsh training only made me weak and thin to a point that I was only bones and skin. I didn't reach any enlightenment, and it was a very wasteful action."

What does the "holding breath" technique do to you? Everyone knows that if you forcefully stop the breath you suffocate and die. What happens if we hold our breath intentionally?

Summarizing the Buddha's story, if you block the doorways of the air such as the mouth and nose, air starts to flow through the ears, accompanied by loud noise and pain. If you block the ears, it will cause a pain like something smashing your head or slashing your stomach. If you continue further, it will feel as if your entire body is heated and burnt.

After repeating such experiences, Buddha quit the training, believing that such training methods and techniques of extreme asceticism would not lead to enlightenment.

By observing the breath, he came to understand a valuable lesson that nobody had yet realized. At that point, he began teaching his disciples a meditation method that focused on observing of breath in order to realize and understand the more subtle states of mind. As stated in the sutra, which, is depicted in the ancient Buddhist text of *Samyutta Nikaya*."

OBSERVE YOUR OWN BREATH

Observing the breath is an important key in the type of meditation called *Vippassana,* which Buddha is supposed to have practiced.

Your respiratory organs function subconsciously, like other organs such as the heart, stomach, intestines, or liver. However, one major difference is that, unlike others, they can be controlled intentionally. In other words, to a certain point we can control our respiratory organs through our intention, just like our hands or feet.

Let's begin observing the breath. You can start by doing this for only a few minutes a day. Sit in a chair relaxed with your back straight, close your eyes gently or keep them half open, and bring your attention to your breath. You can of course do this lying on your back, but it's more likely that you'll fall asleep that way so it may be better to sit in a chair. However, if you'd like to, you can practice this lying down before going to bed at night so you can fall asleep quickly.

Don't try to breathe longer or more deeply. Just observe the way your natural breath is. When you're just starting, it may be better to observe how your chest or stomach moves as you breathe.

Then observe how the air travels through your nose. By "observe," I don't mean that you observe by looking into a mirror, of course. Your eyes should be lightly closed. To observe here means to focus your consciousness on something and carefully verify it. Observe the doorway of the breath carefully, as if you have gatekeepers at the nostrils watching how many and what kinds of people are entering the gates, and who is going out.

You will undoubtedly realize that it is fairly difficult to focus your mind even during just one breath without being distracted by other matters.

If you acknowledge what you are doing every time you breathe, you will gradually focus for longer periods of time.

You may find yourself thinking about something else when you're supposed to be focusing your mind on your breath. For example, you may start wondering if tonight's baseball game is still on when you hear the sound of rain. Even if you're not distracted by a sound or a voice, you may find yourself thinking about what to have for dinner, or whether you've left the kettle on the stove. This kind of motion of the mind is called "cluttered thoughts." If you haven't trained your mind, it's natural to have cluttered thoughts, so don't worry and just go back to focusing on your breath again if you notice that your mind is chattering. Gradually, you will observe your breath for longer without losing your focus. You're not observing your breath just to learn what your breath is like. It may seem strange, but our mind naturally calms down when we bring our attention to the breath.

You might find that the same thought keeps coming up no matter how hard you try to focus on your breath. That might feel fine if it's a positive thought, but if it's a negative emotion such as a complaint, a grudge, or hatred, it can poison you. It is of course impossible to resolve all problems, but it is important to acknowledge that there are some negative emotions hidden in the depth of your heart like lumps. If you observe this state of your mind, the lumps can become smaller or disappear.

When you observe your breath, you may realize that your bad posture is interfering with your breath, or you may find a subtle pain in your body that you wouldn't feel otherwise. When this happens, correct your posture by slowly adjusting your body so you can breathe more deeply. I think you'll feel better and it will be easier for you to breathe.

When you observe your breath, you will become aware of your physical and mental condition, and this will lead to a better state. I'd like you to take the time to engage in this, even if only for ten minutes a day.

ENHANCE YOUR ABILITY TO CONCENTRATE AND RELAX BY BREATHING

Concentration and relaxation—these are both very important in our lives. They seem to be opposites, disassociated with each other, but there is actually a very deep connection.

When you're too nervous, you tend to get stiff and can't concentrate; in other words, in order to concentrate you have to be relaxed. At the same time, when you're focused, you also experience profound relaxation, so it's better to think of concentration and relaxation as a double-faced ability.

Let's talk about relaxation first. Even when you lie down and think you're relaxed, there is a great deal of tension and stiffness left in your body. Imagine that there's a much deeper relaxation than what you've experienced. If you assume you're not tense, you can't achieve deeper relaxation.

There's no limit to the depth of relaxation. You can lead yourself to deeper relaxation through breathing and guided relaxation techniques. When you're relaxed, your cerebrum emits α-waves or θ-waves. This is when you get more inspiration, ideas, and intuitions free from preconceptions. It creates a foundation upon which to exercise your abilities to work or study, and to enhance your health and spirit. Ten minutes of this is comparable to one hour of sleep.

Now let's think about concentration. Do you ever feel like taking a break after you concentrate on something? That's because you subconsciously hold your breath when you concentrate, resulting in a lack of oxygen in the brain. Your brain gets exhausted because it lacks and needs oxygen but is still working very hard as you concentrate.

If you believe that you still have tomorrow, your concentration on the "here and now" diminishes. In order to make your subconscious cooperate with you, you must believe that you are fighting with your back to the wall. If you work unwillingly or hesitantly, you won't be able to focus even if you're good at it. It's important to commit to work with joy and willingness.

When you're vulnerable under pressure, it's because the tension you feel at the thought that you have to do something is interfering with your concentration. You need to train yourself to focus on believing that you are doing the best you can do, no matter what the circumstances are—that even if the result is not what you expected, it matters that you did your best.

Practicing breathing techniques won't suddenly turn you into a totally different person who can concentrate. If you focus on things with an empty mind in general, you will naturally start concentrating.

To enhance your concentration ability, you need to concentrate on every little thing in your life by breathing out slowly. When you eat, don't watch TV or read newspapers, but bring your focus to chewing and tasting, and try to harmonize your body, mind, and breath. If you can concentrate for a little while, stretch your body to take a deep breath and don't wear out your brain.

Note that there is a difference between concentration, in which you collect *Ki* with your intention, and attachment, in which your mind is distracted by something and your energy focused on that something.

SUTRA RECITATION BREATHING TECHNIQUE:
THE SECRET OF LONGEVITY OF MONKS

Traditionally it is said that monks tend to live a longer life. Let's take a look at this. Their disciplined way of living or diet may be part of the reason, or could it be a reward for their faith? They may be stress-free because they learn to stabilize their minds by studying the teachings of Buddha. It is also said that your breath becomes deeper and longer when you recite sutra, resulting in longevity.

But reciting sutra doesn't always make your breath longer. Whenever I have an opportunity to attend Buddhist gatherings, I try to pay attention to the various ways that monks recite. I observe what kind of breath they take, or how they pause to get their breath as they recite.

Most of the time, I find that they have a nice voice but that their breath isn't long enough. Rarely is there someone with long breath who has a beautiful voice that vibrates in the stomach. I suspect that these results differ based on their intentions— whether they view recitation as a breathing practice or just a duty.

Once I stayed at the house of a follower of some religious group who recites sutra every day as a spiritual routine. However, his breath was not very long. He didn't seem to pay much attention to the breathing aspect of the recitation. It's wonderful that he recites sutra every day, but I thought that his physical and mental health would both be better if he intentionally added a breathing practice to his recitation.

Practicing inhaling and exhaling the air can be effective to a certain point, but it's definitely not enough to just make your breath longer. If you don't exercise enough or have tension in your shoulders or chest, you cannot make the most of your ability to breathe.

As far as I have observed, monks in sects who conduct daily prayers with movements such as *Gotaitouchi*—the greatest salute in Buddhism, in which you put your knees, elbows, and head on the ground and put your hands together to worship—usually have longer breath and their voices travel farther during recitation. To deepen your breath, you need to practice methods that keep your body flexible.

It is said that the Fourteenth Dalai Lama, the international Buddhist leader, spends at least two hours a day practicing *Gotaitouchi* several dozen times and reciting. It seems that Tibetan monks including His Holiness have long breath.

Let me briefly explain some Chanting Breathing Exercises. I'll explain the method using the Heart Sutra as an example, but you can use any kind of sutra.

CHANTING BREATHING EXERCISE POSTURE

Sit in *Seiza* form, in which you sit on your heels. Don't cross your feet as this makes your pelvis tilt to the front and back or left and right. Align the first joints of your big toes, open the ankles, and place your butt on them. Keep your knees about one or two fists apart so that you can breathe more easily. Stick out your butt and sit your spine straight up on your pelvis. If you can't sit in *Seiza* form, sit with your legs bent in front, leaning on a small cushion or towel placed right at the tailbone. This makes your spine straight.

Lift your chest slightly. Pull your chin in slightly and lift your head up as if it's being pulled by a string. Don't let the neck or shoulders tense up and stretch out your shoulders to the side.

Hold the script with both hands in front of your chest. Keep the fingers straight up and hold the script with your thumbs and pinkies in front and the other three fingers in back. Hold it gently a little lower than eye height. Holding it this way, you don't need as much force as you would if you held it with your thumbs and index fingers; therefore, your arms, shoulders, neck, and throat do not need to be tensed, making it easier to vocalize.

BREATHING, VOCALIZING, AND BEING CONSCIOUS

Inhale through your nose quickly (in about 0.5 seconds), and as you exhale, try to vocalize as many letters or syllables as possible until you exhale all the breath, maintaining the breathing rhythm.

The Heart Sutra consists of approximately 270 Chinese characters, depending on the version of the translation. If it takes you a second to read each letter, it will take about four and a half minutes to finish reading. Maintain a reading speed of one letter per second, or fifteen letters in ten seconds at the most, which would take about three minutes to finish.

Pronounce each letter clearly. For a greater effect, repeat it three times consecutively. When you read it for the second time, try to read more letters in one breath than you did the first time.

When you vocalize, try to let the sound out from the bottom of your stomach rather than from your throat or chest, vibrating the sound in your entire body. Beginners tend to tighten their throats when they vocalize. Try to vocalize while pushing the air out with your stomach.

Your stomach naturally goes in when you laugh, so the key to doing this is to act as if you're laughing. But note that when you laugh, you inhale each time you go "ha ha ha." When you chant, you have to keep exhaling until you breathe out all the air.

Keep your focus on the sound of your voice—become the sound itself, and let it vibrate throughout your body. This will be good training in concentrating your mind, and will be helpful in learning about *Ki*.

There are a number of English translations of the Heart Sutra. You can chant the English version in the same manner more or less, trying to vocalize as many syllables as your breath allows.

Heart Sutra

MA KA HAN NYA HA RA MIT TA SHIN GYO

KAN JI ZAI BO SATSU GYOJIN HAN NYA HA RA MIT TA JI SHOKEN
GO ON KAI KODO

ITS SAI KOYAKU SHA RI SHI SHIKI FU I KO KOFU I SHIKI SHIKI
SOKU ZE KO

KOSOKU ZE SHIKI JOSOGYOSHIKI YAKU BU NYO ZE SHA RI SHI ZE
SHO HOKOSO

FU SHOFU METSU FU KU FU JO   FU ZOFU GEN   ZE KO KOCHO
MU SHIKI MU JU

SOGYOSHIKI MU GEN NI BI ZES SHIN I MU SHIKI SHOKOMI
SOKU HO MU GEN KAI NAI

SHI MU I SHIKI KAI MU MU MYO YAKU MU MU MYOJIN   NAI SHI
MU ROSHI YAKU MU

ROSHI JIN MU KU SHOMETSU DO MU CHI YAKU MU TOKU I MU
SHO TOKU KO BO DAI

SAT TA   E HAN NYA HA RA MIT TA KO   SHIN MU KEI GE MU KEI
GE KO   MU U

KU FU   ON RI ITS SAI TEN DOMU SO KU KYONE HAN SAN ZE
SHO BUTSU E HAN

NYA HA RA MIT TA KO TOKU A NOKU TA RA SAN MYAKU SAN BO
DAI KO CHI HAN NYA HARA

MIT TA   ZE DAI JIN SHU   ZE DAI MYOSHU ZE MU JOSHU   ZE MU
TODOSHU

NOJO ITS SAI KU   SHIN JITSU FU KO KO SETSU HAN NYA HA RA
MIT TA SHU SOKU SETSU

SHU WATSU

GYA TEI GYA TEI HA RA GYA TEI HARA SO GYA TEI

BO JI SOWA KA HAN NYA SHIN GYO

HEART SUTRA TRANSLATION

The highest knowledge is to understand the nature of supreme wisdom.

*He whose spirit has attained the satori state (enlightenment) and who sees
the truth comes to understand, due to this profound wisdom, that the body,
the mind, and all that exist are only apparent manifestations. Then he is
liberated from all suffering and calamity.*

*Thus the body is only a transitory manifestation and is the activities of the
mind such as feelings, ideas, desire, and ego.*

*All that exists comes from the infinite. Therefore, there is really no creation,
no destruction, no purification, no impurity, no progressing, no regressing.
Thus in the world of eternity there is no body, no senses, no avidity, no ego,
no eyes, no ears, no nose, no tongue, no flesh, no desires, no colors, no voice,
no scent, no taste, no thoughts, no visible world, no experience, no blind
instinct, no death due to age, no end of death due to age, no anxiety, no
bonds, no piece of mind, no discipline, no knowledge, no acquirements. He
who lives in satori and is seeking only truth does not encumber his mind*

with obsessions, because he has found freedom in this world through this supreme wisdom. If one has no fixed ideas, one does not know fear. If one does not know fear, one can be detached from every illusion and every bad thought and live in sacred joy forever. He who understands the world of present-past-future eternity, thanks only to that wisdom, can receive the sacred and universal knowledge. It is from that supreme wisdom that the magic formula reveals nothing other than simple truth and liberates us from all suffering. Here is my interpretation of the teaching of this wonderful wisdom.

"Knowledge and Action." "Understand and Do."

Only the unification of knowledge and doing contains simple truth.

EKOBUN

May the wisdom of this sutra have good effects for all beings, so that
all of us can go the way to enlightenment.

BEST SELLER OF THE EDO PERIOD?
HAKUIN'S BREATHING TECHNIQUE

If you research the roots of Japanese abdominal breathing techniques, or *Tanden* breathing techniques, one of the methods you will encounter is the Buddhist way of harmonizing the breath. In Zen Buddhist training, harmonizing body, breath, and mind is very important, and harmonizing the breath is the most essential. Buddhism was introduced to Japan during the sixth century in the Nara Period, so we can assume that the breathing technique to balance breath, body, and mind has been practiced since then.

The most famous practitioner is a Zen Buddhist named Ekaku Hakuin (1685–1768), who described breathing techniques in relation to physical and mental health matters. Hakuin is the founder of the *Rinzai* sect. In his books *Yasenkanwa* and *Orategama*, he handed down the Inner Observation Method and *Nanso* Meditation, based on *Zazen* breathing techniques that helped him heal disease. Since then, the practice of these breathing techniques for health, longevity, and healing became very popular in Japan

Hakuin was born in 1685, into a family that operated an inn. He was innately physically weak but very mature spiritually that at the age of seven he surprised everyone by memorizing the Hokke Sutra, which he heard at a temple.

At age 15, he became a monk at Harano Shoin-Ji Temple. He left the temple at age 19, and searched all over Japan for a master to study with. He became enlightened at the age of 24, but he kept training because he realized he was inadequate.

However, when he was about 26 years old he became ill from the harsh training, which weakened his nerves to the point where he was almost dying. It seems that he suffered from a very serious neurosis, combined with tuberculosis.

He tried herbs and acupuncture, but could not get any better. Then he heard about a master named Hakuyushi, who lived in a cave in Mt. Shirakawa, at the bottom of Mt. Hiei in Yamashiro, Kyoto. Hakuin went to visit him and learned *Naikan* Method, or the Secret of Seeing the Inner Self from the master, which changed his life forever.

At the age of 73, Hakuin handed down the secret method that he learned from the master in his book *Yasen Kanwa*. Since his books are easy to read, the method became popular.

Hakuin regarded the technique that the master handed down to him as "a secret teaching of longevity, to cultivate *Ki*, nurture the spirit, and restore one's life-force energy." In other words, he regarded it as a secret method for health and longevity, to enrich the mind and body by cultivating *Ki*, spiritual and physical power.

Let me explain the Naikan Method briefly. According to Hakuin's teaching, you should relax without thinking of anything and sleep deeply before you start. Then, when you are half asleep or half awake, stretch your legs out together. Hakuin didn't mention anything about hands or arms, but I think it would be a good idea to stretch them out, with your hands held together, as you stretch your legs. When you forcefully stretch out the tense and contracted body and let it loose, *Ki* will flow better in the body. I also think that it's effective to stretch your legs, pushing out your heels in order to stretch your Achilles tendons.

As you breathe out, imagine you're releasing your energy, strengthening *tanden*, and filling your lower body with *Ki*, especially to the center of your feet, and repeatedly recite the following Naikan Method as if hypnotizing yourself.

1. Waga kono kikaitanden, youkyaku sokushin, masanikore waga honrai no menboku, menboku nanino bikouka aru.

2. Waga kono kikaitanden, masani kore waga honbun no kakiyou, kakiyou nanino shousokuka aru.

3. Waga kono kikaitanden, masani kore waga yuishin no jodo, jodo nanino sogonka aru.

4. Waga kono kikaitanden, masani kore waga koshin no mida, mida nanino howoka toku.

These are their meanings:

1. The actual me is this *Kikaitanden* and *Youkyakusokushin* (pelvis, legs, feet, heart), and the actual me doesn't exist in nostrils.

2. My actual home is this *Kikaitanden,* and this is my home.

3. My *Kikaitanden* is the paradise, and there is no other paradise where we can go to decorate elaborately.

4. My *Kikaitanden* is myself who is perfect, where Amida resides, and there will be no Amida's teachings away from here.

In short, he's emphasizing that you can balance yourself if you bring your focus to *Kikaitanden* and *Youkyakusyokushin* and lower your *Ki* to the lower body. He also talks about the importance of collecting *Ki,* or life force energy, to *Kikaititanden.* If you find the words of the Naikan Method difficult, you can recite the modern translation instead. It's important to repeat the breathing, with a belief that *Tanden* is very important.

Kikaitanden is below your navel. "*Tan*" of *Tanden* is the medicine of immortality in Taoism, and "*Den*" means a place to cultivate it. In China, there are three different *Tandens* (or *Tan Tiens*): upper (the center of the head), middle (the center of the chest), and lower (below the stomach), but in Japan the lower one is called *Tanden. Kikaitanden* also indicates this lower *Tanden.* It is said that it resides at the center of a triangle that connects the navel, the lumber 3, and the anus. But, of course, it's not something you can see even if you cut your body open.

TENDAI TAISHI: THE ROOT OF JAPANESE BREATHING METHODS

If you trace the practice that Hakuin copied, which taught people about the relationship between breath, body and mind, your search will end at Tendai Taishi Chigi (538-597), the founder of the Chinese Tendai Sect.

I've always wondered why there's a difference between the breathing method practiced in Southern Buddhism (Sri Lanka or Myanmar, for example), such as in *Anapanasatti* and *Vippassana*, and that of Japanese Buddhism such as *Zazen*. In Japan or China, we emphasize the importance of focusing on *Tanden* as you correct your breath. In Southern Buddhism, on the other hand, they emphasize using the breath for meditation to set the mind and observe every moment of reality. We don't know which Buddhist discipline Shakyamuni Buddha taught his students 2,500 years ago. However, it is clear that the practice of Japanese Buddhism became different from that of Southeast Asia because it was introduced to Japan through China.

At any rate, it is true that there have been many great Zen monks, thanks to the Buddhist philosophy and the practices of Buddhist discipline that were introduced to China from India, especially that of Chigi Tendai Taishi. If you were to trace it, the model for many Japanese Zen monks would lead back to the teachings of Tendai Taishi.

Tendai Taishi's books are still available. One of them is *Tendai Shoshikan*. It is famous as the oldest written material in Buddhist history that preaches in detail how to meditate and how the mind works. *Zazen* practitioners after Tendai Taishi, including the famous Zen monk called Dogen, used this book as the foundation of their practice.

Let me introduce an important passage from *Tendai Shoshikan* regarding a breathing technique necessary before doing *Zazen*. It might be difficult to understand this old Japanese phrase, but briefly, here's what it's all about. It means "exhale out through open mouth the *Jaki*, or negative *Ki*, that is blocking the energy canals (meridians) throughout the body. If you imagine you're releasing *Jaki*, it will go out. When you exhale it out completely, close your mouth and breathe in clean *Ki* through your nose." This is the very same technique that we practice in yoga, called cleansing breath technique. I'm not sure whether it originated in India or

China, but it's important to change *Ki* before you do breathing practice for *Zazen*.

Tendai Taishi classifies ways of breathing into four categories, as follows. "There are four phases in harmonizing your breath. Firstly wind, secondly gasping, thirdly *Ki*, and finally breath. The former three are regarded as disharmonized phases, and the last as a harmonizing phase."

The wind phase is a breath in which the air makes a noise like wind as it goes in and out. Because only rough breathing makes a noise like this, you can't expect to calm your mind with this.

The gasping phase is literally a gasping breath. Although it doesn't make any noise, it's a breath in which you suffer. It doesn't calm your mind, but instead creates disturbing emotions.

The *Ki* phase is a breath that has no rhythm or gracefulness. Most people use this one to breathe in their normal daily lives. Again, this is not a quiet breath that calms your mind.

Then what is breath breathing like? I'd like to quote the words of Tendai Taishi. "The 'breath' phase doesn't make noise or stagnate, and is not rough, but is as soft as cotton when it goes in, where you are relaxed and don't know if you are really breathing or not." It is a state in which you are peaceful and calm in both body and mind, and you feel subtle joy springing inside of you.

According to Tendai Taishi, we must follow three principles in order to breathe with this phase of breath. The three principles are

1. Stabilize your mind in the lower area.
2. Relax your body.
3. Imagine that *Ki* goes in and out of the pores and there's nothing to stop the flow.

The lower area indicated in the first principle is *Tanden*. If you bring your attention to *Tanden* to breathe, your mind calms down and your breath will be harmonized. The second principle is to relax the tension in the shoulders and neck, relaxing the upper body. The third principle is not a physical breath that moves your chest or abdomen, but a state in which your entire body becomes one, and *Ki* is going in and out of all your powers. In this breath, you will feel natural and good and be stable physically and mentally.

Chapter 4
EXERCISES
Characteristics of the Tatsumura Breathing Method

I believe that we can only understand ourselves when we take a look at the layers of our existence, such as our physical body, *Ki* in us, and the mind, in a holistic way. I feel the same way about our breath.

The Tatsumura Method is organized to work on body, *Ki*, and mind from a holistic point of view; therefore, it is very helpful in developing your hidden gifts and abilities. Its goal is not only to improve your physical health, but also to enhance and strengthen your whole sense of being.

The method is a mixture of the beneficial aspects of traditional Eastern teachings such as yoga, *Chi Gong*, *Sendo* (a Taoist training to become an immortal hermit), Shinto, and other traditional Japanese breathing techniques, combined with a scientific point of view to make it easy to understand. I can't introduce every single exercise I created, but I picked the ones that anyone can easily practice, regardless of their age or sex.

This method is good for busy people because it can be practiced on the train, as you walk, or before you go to sleep.

I divide these practices into **three major categories**.

The first is a technique that uses movement to deepen the breath.

There are three different kinds of exercises in this category:

- **Breathing Exercises**, which work on the physical level
- **Tree Breathing Technique**, which works on the Ki level
- **Spine Shaking Breathing Technique**, which works on the mind.

I'd like you to spontaneously practice them whenever you have time, even if it's not every day.

Please refrain from practicing these right after you eat or when you're not in good physical condition, such as when you're sick or injured. Observe your condition and practice without straining.

In the second category are practices of different breathing techniques Abdominal breathing, total breathing, cleansing breathing, *Tanden* breathing, *Shikofumi* breathing, and spine twisting breathing. These will be more effective if you practice any breathing exercises or the tree breathing technique beforehand. If you learn the correct way to breathe, your breath will be deeper and slower.

In the third category are practical techniques you can use when you face life events, to calm yourself down, or to persuade someone, and so on. These are helpful in our daily lives or in business fields. You should practice these repeatedly so that you can remember and use them whenever necessary.

FOR DEEPER BREATH 1
BREATH FOR THE PHYSICAL BODY
BREATHING EXERCISES

The foundation of breathing techniques is the practice of physical exercises that enhance the flexibility of the respiratory system muscles and correct distortion in bones associated with breathing, such as the ribs and shoulder blades. Yoga or *Qi Gong* play a role in this.

I'd like to introduce some breathing exercises from the Tatsumura Method that are effective but still easy for beginners.

While these require physical movement, please remember that the main purpose is not physical exercise. The important thing is to breathe and let *Ki* flow with the postures.

1. Do not practice for at least two hours after you eat.

2. Don't worry if you can't follow the instructions perfectly. These aren't physical exercises but breathing techniques. It's more important that you breathe in the posture.

3. If an exercise makes you feel sick, stop and take a rest.

4. If an exercise makes you feel better, recognize that it's something you need. Practice it knowing that.

5. If you are seeing a doctor or in a hospital, please consult with your doctor before practicing these.

ARM TWISTING

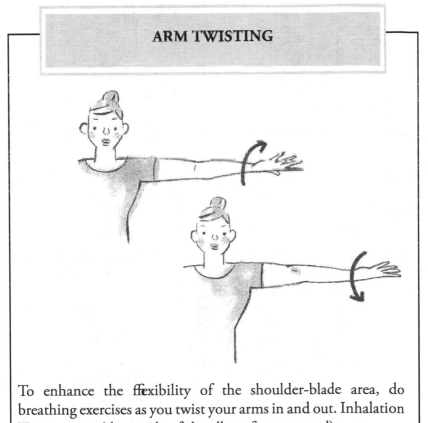

To enhance the flexibility of the shoulder-blade area, do breathing exercises as you twist your arms in and out. Inhalation Twisting out (the inside of the elbow faces upward)

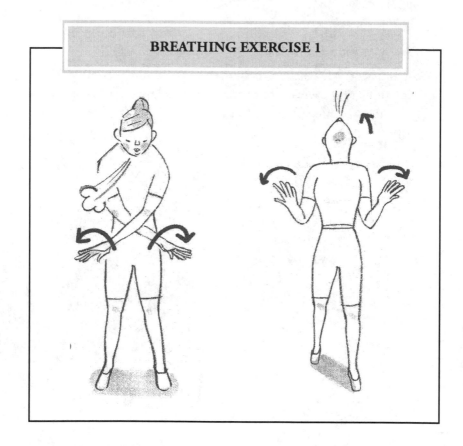

BREATHING EXERCISE 1: STRETCHING YOUR CHEST MUSCLES FRONT AND BACK

1. Keeping your feet shoulder-width apart, cross your arms in front of your body as you exhale, tilting forward and contracting your abdomen. Twist your arms out as you exhale completely.

2. Step out with your left foot as you inhale, bending and pulling your arms back by your sides and pushing your chest out as you lean back.

3. Inhale, twisting your wrist out, then bring your foot back to the original position as you exhale, crossing your arms and twisting them in as you finish exhaling.

BREATHING EXERCISE 2:
STRETCHING YOUR CHEST MUSCLES RIGHT AND LEFT

1. Keeping your feet shoulder-width apart, stretch your arms out horizontally to the side. Bend your upper body to the left as you exhale. Bend your right elbow and twist the arm in as you bring it up from the hip to the armpit. Reach out your left arm to the flow and twist it in, exhaling completely. Keep your face down.

2. Bring your upper body up as you inhale, stretching your arms out horizontally to the side. Open your chest as if you were stretching to the side and twist your arms out, exhaling completely.

*Do the same movements, bending your body to the right. Each time you bend your body to the right or left is counted as one. Do this ten times.

BREATHING EXERCISE 3:
TWISTING AND EXPANDING THE RIBCAGE

1. Keep your feet shoulder-width apart. Bring your arms up in front and twist them out.

2. Twist your body and arms to the right as you exhale, twisting the arms in and exhaling completely. Try to twist your upper body as far as you can, father than the middle.

3. Bring your body back to the front as you inhale, twisting your stretched arms out as you finish inhaling.

4. Bring your arms down as you exhale, then bring them up again as you inhale. Twist them out and finish inhaling.

BREATHING EXERCISE 3

BREATHING EXERCISE 4:
STRETCHING YOUR CHEST MUSCLES UP AND DOWN

1. Keep your feet shoulder-width apart. Cross your arms in front of your body as you exhale. Bend forward slightly and contract your abdomen, twisting your arms in and exhaling completely.

2. As you inhale, take a big step forward with your right foot, stretching your arms up in an angle and bending back to look up at the sky. Twist your wrists out and finish inhaling.

3. Bring your foot and body back to the center as you exhale. Cross your arms as you did in step one, twisting them in and exhaling completely.

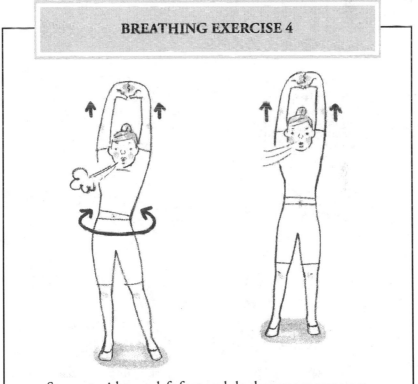

BREATHING EXERCISE 4

Step out with your left foot and do the same movements.
Each time you bend back is counted as one. Do this ten times.

BREATHING EXERCISE 5

Do both sides at least two times before resting your arms.

BREATHING EXERCISE 5:

STRETCHING THE ABDOMINAL AREA

1. Keep your feet shoulder-width apart and keep your arms up, interlacing your fingers with the palms facing up as you inhale.

2. As you exhale, draw a big circle twice with your hip, with your belly button at the center. Do the same thing as you inhale. Repeat on the left side.

FOR DEEPER BREATH 2 BREATHING
TO BALANCE *KI*:

TREE BREATHING METHOD

This is a breathing technique to enhance the entry and exit of *Ki* energy, the fflow of *Ki*, and the balance of *Ki*. You are practicing primarily to control *Ki*. The exercises use basic movements from *Qi Gong* and some visualization.

It is our visual image that leads us to move *Ki*. We can achieve not only physical effects but also those of *Ki* by practicing this well.

I call the technique I'm about to introduce in this section the "Tree Breathing Method" because you use it you guide and move *Ki* by visual izing your body as a tree.

Once, around 1988 or 1989, when I was the director of the Oki Yoga Dojo, I was searching for a place to meditate on the mountain in preparation for an afternoon class at the Shimoda Training Center. I found a spot on a slope filled with cedars and cypress. I had a good feeling about the place. I picked a relatively big cypress tree, and began trying to correct my breath in order to do standing Zen meditation about three feet away from the tree.

It was a very quiet place with no disturbance from other people, because only the owners usually came there. I started to feel the energy of the cypress in front of me, and my mind magically began to calm down. I heard the birds singing too. I had done standing meditation numerous times before, but this was my first time standing still in front of a tree in meditation.

As I meditated, I felt like stretching my right arm back over my shoulder, so I did. I also felt like stretching my left arm in a different direction. I thought it was strange because, even though my arms were stretched over my shoulders, they didn't get tired.

A little while later, I remembered that I needed to go back, so I slowly opened my eyes to look up at the tree. I was taken by surprise. The cypress had two big branches spreading to the right and left, and I realized that the position of my arms was like that of the branches. That was the first time I realized that my body could synchronize with trees.

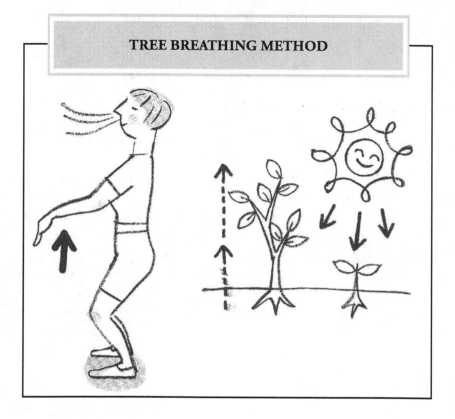

TREE BREATHING METHOD

Soon after that, in 1993, I learned about Master Lin's *Taichi 18 Movements* and began to study it on videotape. In 1996, the master came to my teaching center, Space Gaia Symphony, to lead a workshop. I studied directly with him, and he gave me permission to instruct the first and second of the eighteen sets. The Tree Breathing Method is an application of the first of the eighteen sets, but it was my own idea to make it resemble the image of a growing tree. That is something I developed through my interactions with trees, like the one I had in Shimoda.

The Tree Breathing Method will be more effective if you imagine that YOU are a TREE. If you do this exercise without visualization, you may gain the physical effects, but not *Ki*. You don't have to move exactly as instructed. The important thing is to visualize as you breathe. Don't get caught up in the movements when you practice.

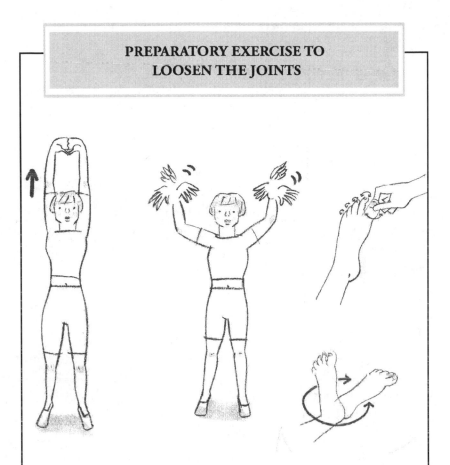

- Stretch your arms together as you exhale
- Shake your hands as you exhale.
- Rotate your feet as you exhale.
- Rotate your toes as you exhale.

Before you practice the six breathing methods, you should move your fingers, feet, wrists, ankles, and all the joints of the body to make the exercises more effective.

TREE BREATHING TECHNIQUE 1:

ASCENDING TO THE SKY, DESCENDING TO THE LAND

Let's begin with the first step. Trees receive *Ki*, such as sunlight, from the sky, and grow toward that direction after sprouting from a seed. At the same time, they grow deep into the earth to search for water and nutrition in the ground. If you meditate standing quietly in front of a tree and try to feel its energy, you will be able to feel these two different movements of energy flowing upward and downward.

1. Keep your feet shoulder-width apart and keep the fifth toes parallel. Bend your knees slightly and let your hands hang by your thighs. Imagine you are a young tree, with your feet as the roots and your torso as the trunk.

2. Inhale and, with your palms facing down, lift your hands up as if they are being pushed by a force from below. As you straighten your knees, bring your hands up to the height of your head and finish inhaling. Shift your awareness from the bottom of your feet to your knees, thighs, lower abdomen, chest, neck, and head, visualizing the energy of the earth being absorbed through the bottom of your feet and ascending through the trunk to the top of the tree.

3. As you exhale, lower your hands as if they were something heavy slowly sinking down into the water. Finish exhaling as you bend your knees and bring your hands down to the sides of your thighs. Shift your awareness from your head to your face, chest, belly, thighs, knees, and the bottom of your feet, visualizing the energy of the sun flowing down from the tip of the tree to the trunk.

TREE BREATHING TECHNIQUE 1
ASCENDING TO THE SKY, DESCENDING TO THE LAND

Repeat this up-and-down movement eight times.
Imagine the tree grow ing bigger each time.

TREE BREATHING TECHNIQUE 2
STRETCHING BRANCHES AND EXPANDING ROOTS

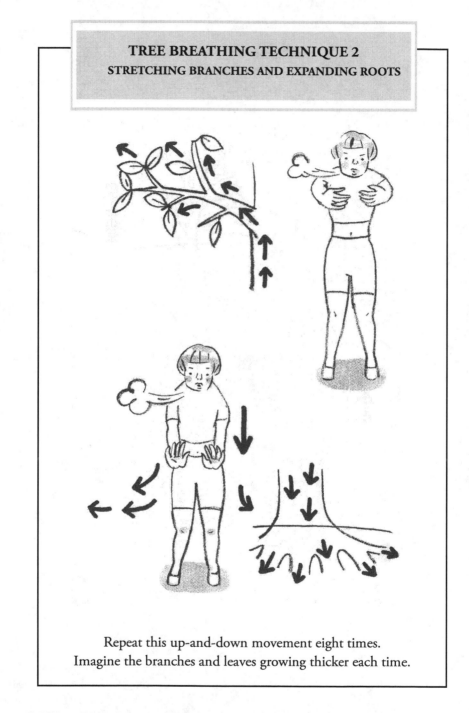

Repeat this up-and-down movement eight times.
Imagine the branches and leaves growing thicker each time.

TREE BREATHING TECHNIQUE 2:
STRETCHING BRANCHES AND EXPANDING ROOTS

Trees not only grow toward the sky but also expand their branches and leaves to the sides to absorb as much *Ki* from the sun as possible. Likewise, their roots grow not only deep into the ground but also to the sides.

When you quietly meditate standing in front of a tree, you can feel its *Ki* expanding to the sides.

1. Stand in the same position that you took at the beginning of exercise one. Imagine that you have become a slightly bigger young tree, with your feet as the roots, torso as the trunk, and arms as the branches. As you inhale, lift up your arms with your palms facing down and straighten your knees. Bring your arms up as if you were a tree growing toward the sky, and when your arms are at the height of your chest, open them as if you were holding a ball of air that keeps expanding. Open your chest wide and finish inhaling. Shift your awareness from the bottoms of your feet to your knees, thighs, lower abdomen, chest, upper arms, lower arms, wrists, palms, and fingers, imagining the energy of the earth entering through your feet, ascending through the trunk, and reaching the leaves through the branches.

2. As you exhale, slowly bring your arms together, letting them draw toward each other. When they are in front of your chest, lower your hands and bend your knees to sink down. When your hands are by your thighs, finish exhaling and open them to the sides.

   Shift your awareness from your fingertips to your lower arms, upper arms, chest, belly, thighs, knees, and the bottoms of your feet, imagining the energy of the sun gathered in the trunk through the branches to make the trunk stronger and nourish the roots.

TREE BREATHING TECHNIQUE 3:
FRESH BREEZE SHAKING THE TREE

The right winds give trees opportunities to grow, exercise, and communicate with other trees by exchanging pollen. If there were no wind, trees could not grow strong. In the third step, we practice visualizing a tree shaken by the wind.

1. Stand in the same position that you took at the beginning of exercise one. Imagine that you have become a big tree, with your feet as the roots, your torso as the trunk, and your arms as the braches. As you inhale, lift your arms up and place your palms facing each other over your head. As you exhale, slowly tilt your arms to the right as if you were a tree blown by a wind coming from the left. Pushing your hip to the left shifting your weight slightly to the left leg, and tilt your upper body to the right. Keep your left hand above your head, stretch your right arm to the right, and turn your face toward the right hand's fingers as you finish exhaling. As you inhale, bring your arms back to the center and stretch them upward. Turn your face to the front.

2. As you exhale, tilt your arms to the other side and repeat the same steps. Try to move gracefully and ffexibly as if a tremor were being transmitted from the feet to the torso, arms, and fingertips. Imagine that the whole tree trunk is greatly shaken. After you repeat this movement a few times on both sides, lower your arms and come back to the first posture as you exhale.

TREE BREATHING TECHNIQUE 3
FRESH BREEZE SHAKING THE TREE

Repeat eight times on both sides.

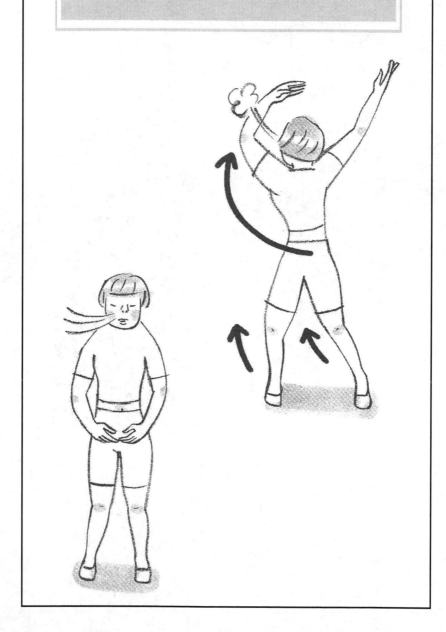

TREE BREATHING TECHNIQUE 4:

TWISTED TRUNK REACHING FOR THE SKY

All trees grow bigger, twisting their trunks even if they might look straight like cedars or cypress. Trees grow stronger against outside forces by twisting themselves.

When I meditate standing in front of a tree, my body sometimes naturally twists like the tree, probably because I synchronize with it.

1. Stand in the same position that you took at the beginning of exercise one. Hold your arms shoulder-width apart and imagine that you are holding a ball of air that size. Imagine yourself as a fast-growing tree, with your feet as the roots, your torso as the trunk, and your arms as the branches.

2. As you exhale, lift your arms up and twist your body slowly, beginning from the hip. Twist and lift your upper body even farther, and stretch your arms to the back and up as you finish exhaling. Bend your knees as you inhale and bring your upper body and arms back to the center position, then twist your body to the other side as you exhale. Finish exhaling as you reach farther back. Breathe in as you come back to the center once again. Repeat this several times and come back to the first position.

TREE BREATHING TECHNIQUE 5:
BIRDS HEALING UNDER THE TREE

Under a tree we not only find fruit, leaves, and protection from strong sunlight, it's also a place that gives life-healing *Ki*. The *Ki* from the tree trunk, big branches, and green leaves gives us comfort, relaxation, and healing energy.

Imagine you have become a large tree, regarded as a mother tree of the forest. Little birds and squirrels hang around under the tree to play and eat the berries. Be grateful for the energy of the sun and the earth that allows you to be alive, and send out the *Ki* of love that allows other small creatures to be alive.

1. Stand in the same position that you took at the beginning of exercise one. Imagine yourself as a very big tree, with your feet as the roots, your torso as the trunk, and your arms as the branches. As you inhale, lightly cross your arms as if you were holding a ball of air, and lift them up.

2. As you finish inhaling, make a circle with your fingers touching each other above your head.

3. As you exhale, stretch your arms to the sides with your fingers pointing out, and slowly bring your arms down. As you bring your arms down, visualize that the lines you draw are the tips of the branches and leaves, and that there are little birds and squirrels playing underneath your arms. As you finish exhaling, cross your arms in front and go back to the movement of step one. Practice this, imagining the cycle of energy, in which the energy from the earth travels through the roots and trunk, and then out to the air through the branches and leaves, finally going back to the earth and reaching the roots again.

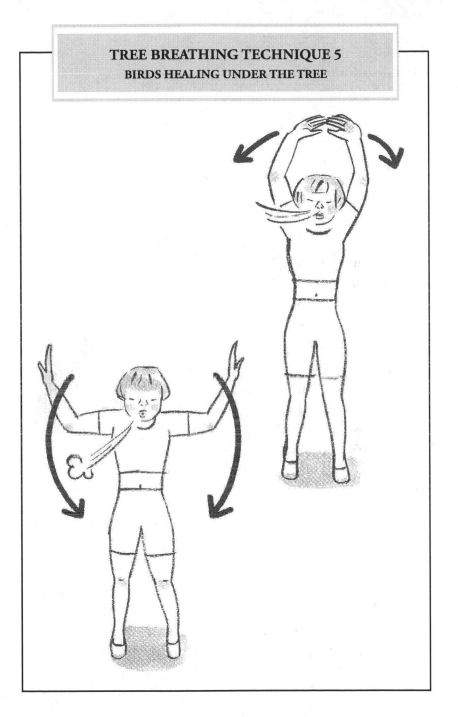

TREE BREATHING TECHNIQUE 5
BIRDS HEALING UNDER THE TREE

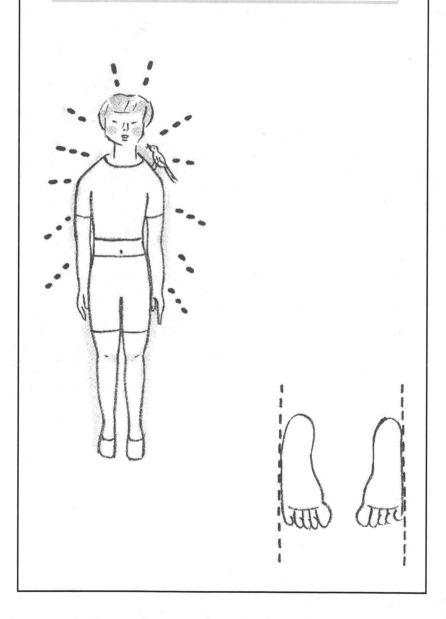

TREE BREATHING TECHNIQUE 6:
STANDING ZEN MEDITATION

You may find as you practice exercises one through five that your muscles don't get tired from standing, because your consciousness is focused on your energetic body. Be a big tree in the forest and meditate standing upright.

Stand in the same position that you took at the beginning of exercise one. Bend your knees slightly and let your hands hang by your sides. Close your eyes and imagine that you're a very big tree in the forest, about one hundred feet tall. Let go of all the tension in your body and breathe naturally. As you inhale, your body expands slightly, and as you exhale, your body shrinks slightly. Imagine that your body is as light as the air, and you're standing supported by the air in each direction. When you look down from the top of the tree, everything looks so small. Little birds come to have berries or to rest on the branches. Imagine that a little bird is resting on your shoulder without any suspicions because it is feeling tree-like *Ki* from you, not human-like *Ki*. If your consciousness is focused on the physical body, your *Ki* will be directed to the tiredness in your feet or your breath, which will make it difficult to stand for a long time.

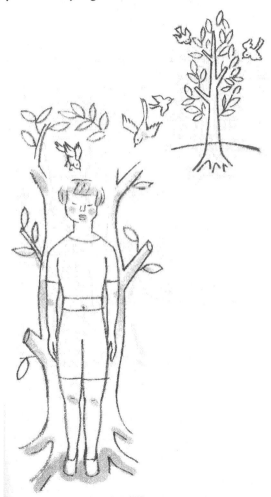

FOR DEEPER BREATH 3
TO CORRECT AN IMBALANCE OF MIND AND BODY: SPINE SHAKING BREATHING TECHNIQUE

Breathing with deep or shallow breaths can cause many different results, but the biggest problem with shallow breathing is that it makes you less sensitive. Our life force naturally seeks a state of easy breathing that makes us feel good. But when, for example, you have a hunched back, you can't breathe properly. If this improper breathing becomes habitual, you become so used to it that you lose your instinct to correct the problem. Your correct natural senses shut down, and you're not able to hear the voice of the life force that wants you to NOT hunch your back, but wants you to return to straight back.

Many of our habitual problems are caused by shallow breathing. On the other hand, if your breath is deep, your senses will be corrected and you'll naturally have good posture, which makes good breathing easy. Your diet will also improve, becoming based on your natural needs, and you'll stop overeating or eating improperly. As a result, you won't be excessively overweight.

Yawning, coughs, and so on, are natural elimination reactions based on our body and our life's needs. They use a different kind of neural path than those used when, for example, your cerebrum sends out the signal to move your arm. They use a path that's meant to correct some kind of imbalance. But this path is rarely used in a very stressful and tense lifestyle—one that creates an imbalance of body and mind and distorts the spine. As a result, you can lose your sensitivity and create an autonomic imbalance.

In most people today, this path is somewhat blocked. It is important that they open it up and regain sensitivity in different aspects of their lives.

Looking at this from the point of view that believes that the force of the universe and life itself sustains life, it is reasonable to say that our spine acts as an antenna to receive this force. Breathing the wrong way distorts the spine, and a distorted spine makes the breath shallower.

In this section, I'll introduce a technique to regain sensitivity in the spine—the antenna—to correctly receive the energy—*Ki,* or *Prana*—which is the vibration of the universe, and which sustains our life. You can practice this anytime you'd like when you have the time.

1. Sideways Rocking Technique

Sit comfortably, whether on the floor in lotus position or on a chair. Close your eyes lightly and slowly start to rock your spine sideways. Keep rocking the way a whip moves, imagining a wave traveling from the base of your spine up to your head. Breathe naturally.

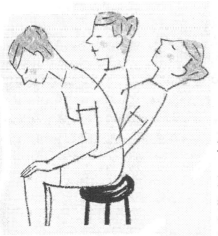

2. Back and Forth Rocking Technique

Rock like a wave traveling back and forth. Drop your head and feel the energy traveling up from your lower abdomen to your stomach, chest, and neck. Then push your chin out and lean forward, pulling your lower back backwards and returning to the original position where your head was dropped. Seen from the side, this movement looks like a wave traveling up through the spine. Breathe naturally.

3. Rotating Technique

Rotate your upper body to the right (or left) with the base of your spine as the center. The base of the spine becomes the tip of a cone, and the circle that you draw with your head becomes the base of the cone. Keep your spine flexible. Using the movements of the wave and the whip, you may draw a more complicated line like a figure 8 or sideways figure 8. When you feel you have done enough, reverse the movement.

4. Free Rocking Technique

As you practice exercises one to three, letting your body move as it wishes, you may find yourself naturally wanting to reverse the movement or move in a different direction. Feel free to move as your body desires. Don't try to control the movements. Let the sensation take control, and stop when you feel like stopping. * Complete exercises one to four in about twenty minutes. Once you've become comfortable with these exercises, you may do just exercise four by itself.

LEARN CORRECT BREATHING TECHNIQUES 1
A Basic Exercise of Abdominal Breathing:
Laughter Breathing

As said in the proverb "Laughter brings fortune to your door," many people have known for a long time that laughing is good for mental and physical health. But that doesn't mean that we always laugh consciously. In the system of yoga founded by Master Masahiro Oki, we have for over fifty years preached a laughing exercise in which breathing technique accompanies conscious laughter.

Norman Cousins made the medical effect of conscious laughter very famous. He was suffering from collagen disease and doctors had given up on him. But conscious laughing miraculously caused him to recover.

It's important to try to create laughter consciously even if nothing is funny. One report, which compared the blood tests of people before and after laughing at a comedy, showed that the macrophages and natural killer cells, indicators of immunity became more active after laughing.

Let's consciously pretend we're laughing. When you laugh, your breath automatically becomes abdominal breath.

1. Sit in a chair with your back straight. Place one hand on the pit of your stomach and the other on the lower abdomen, and breathe in. Then exhale, tilting your upper body forward and laughing "ha ha ha ha ha!" so that the pit becomes deeper as you finish exhaling. When you laugh naturally, you inhale in between each "ha," but you don't in this technique.

2. Straighten your upper body as you inhale through your nose. The key here is to first blow your lower abdomen up big. If you put force into exhaling, you will naturally inhale. * Exhale in five and inhale in one. Repeat this about ten times, relaxing and breathing naturally after each round.

LEARN CORRECT BREATHING TECHNIQUES 2
A BASIC EXERCISE OF ABDOMINAL BREATHING

ABDOMINAL BREATHING ON YOUR BACK (PREPARATION)

If your abdomen is stiff, you can't have deep abdominal breath. In natural Asian treatments, the practitioner always checks the stiffness of your abdomen and treats it to loosen the tension. One cause of abdominal muscle tension can be the legs, especially the thighs. Stiffness in the legs or an imbalance of tension in the muscles at the front, back, inside, or outside can cause bad blood circulation in the organs of the abdominal area, creating tension there as well.

Before you start practicing abdominal breathing, you need to practice leg stretching breathing techniques on the back, sides, and front. If you can't hold your feet without bending your knees, you may find it easier to hold your feet with a towel. However, if you can hold your feet easily, the towel is not necessary.

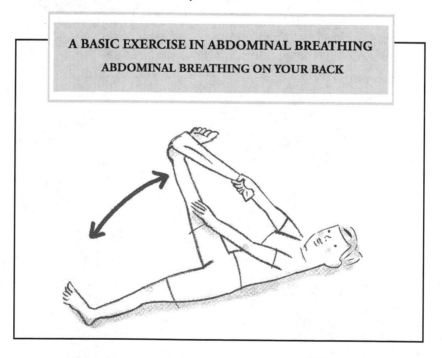

A BASIC EXERCISE IN ABDOMINAL BREATHING

ABDOMINAL BREATHING ON YOUR BACK

BACK-OF-THIGH STRETCHING BREATHING TECHNIQUE

Lift your right leg perpendicular to the ffoor. Put a towel around the feet and hold the towel with your right hand. Your left hand is on the right knee so that your knee does not bend. Your left leg is straight on the ffoor and your upper body and head touch the ffoor. As you exhale, bring your right leg closer to your upper body and stretch the back of the leg, then relax it as you inhale. Repeat this three times. On the fourth time, take several deep breaths with the leg stretched out. Do the same thing with your left leg.

INNER-THIGH STRETCHING BREATHING TECHNIQUE

Lift your right leg and put the towel around your right foot, holding it with your right hand. Your left arm is stretched to the left. As you breathe in and out, slowly drop your right leg to the right. Don't lift your left shoulder or hip away from the ffoor. When it feels open enough, bring it back to center as you breathe in. Repeat this three times. On the fourth time, take several deep breaths with your leg stretched out. Do the same thing with your left leg.

OUTER-THIGH STRETCHING BREATHING TECHNIQUE

Lift your right leg. Put a towel around your feet and hold the towel with your left hand. Stretch your right arm to the right. As you inhale and exhale, drop your right leg to the left. Try not to lift your right shoulder away from the ffoor as you turn your face to the right. When it feels like enough, come back to center as you inhale. Repeat this three times. On the fourth time, take several deep breaths with your leg stretched out. Do the same thing with your left leg.

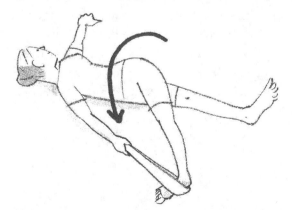

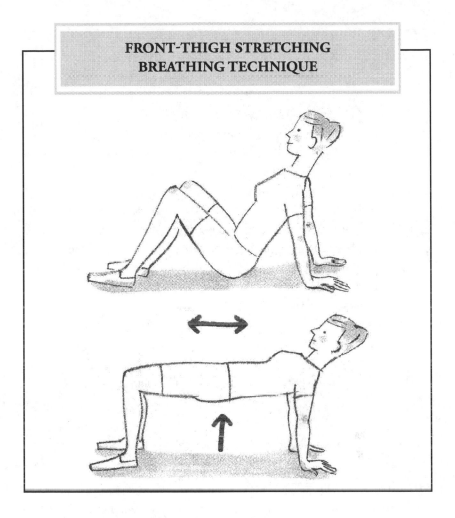

FRONT-THIGH STRETCHING BREATHING TECHNIQUE

Sit on the ffoor with your knees bent, with your feet shoulder-width apart. Lean back with your back at a 45-degree angle to the ffoor and your hands on the ffoor behind your back. Lift your hips till your upper body becomes parallel to the ffoor. Breathe in and push your body forward, then breathe out, stretching the front of the knees. Try to stretch until your knees touch the ffoor, keeping them as close together as possible. Move back as you breathe in, and move forward as you breathe out. Repeat this about ten times.

LEARN CORRECT BREATHING TECHNIQUES 3
A BASIC EXERCISE OF ABDOMINAL BREATHING

ABDOMINAL BREATHING ON YOUR BACK
In this exercise, you breathe in through your nose and out through your mouth. Breathe in as deeply as you can so that the air can reach the alveolus in the lungs. When you breathe out, breathe out slowly as if you are trying to make the flame of a candle fflutter.

Everybody naturally breathes abdominally to a certain point. However, if someone who is not used to this type of breathing tries to do it consciously, they will tend to breathe with their chest, not their abdomen. Therefore, you should start by observing your natural abdominal breathing, and then practice doing it consciously to make it easier to breathe deeply with your abdomen.

If you practice abdominal breathing regularly before you go to sleep, you will fall asleep quickly and deeply. Even when you can't move your body due to disease or injury, you can improve your natural healing power by doing this type of breathing on your back.

1. Lie on your back and place one hand on your chest and the other on your lower abdomen. Observe your abdomen sinking down as you breathe out slowly with your mouth slightly open. If you exhale completely, your abdomen will naturally form a dent without moving your hand on your chest.

2. When you finish exhaling, close your mouth and let go of the tension in your stomach. The air will come in naturally as the muscles move back to their original position. You can tell if you're doing abdominal breathing by the upward movement of your hand on your abdomen. Keep inhaling consciously in accord with the movement of your abdomen, like a balloon expanding. When it's almost full, hold your breath and exhale slowly and consciously.

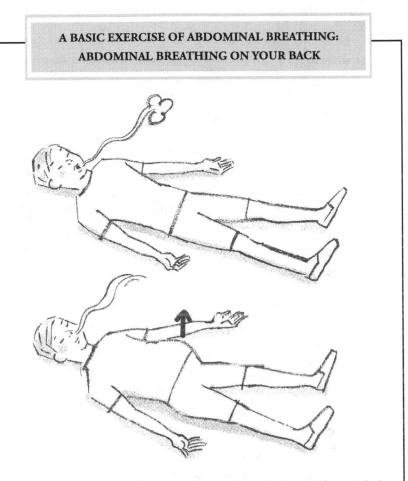

* Breathe in and out for the same number of counts. If you inhale for five seconds, exhale for five seconds too. Once you become used to this type of breathing, you can repeat the exercise with your arms and hands at your side at about a 30-degree angle, palms facing up.

*To increase your awareness of your abdominal movement, it may be helpful to place a book or other object on your abdomen. Be aware as it slowly goes up and down. Once you are used to this type of breathing, breathe out through your nose as well.

CORRECT POSTURE

Before we practice perfect breathing, we need to master correct posture. Whether you're standing up or sitting in a chair, the correct posture is one in which you can breathe deeply, not one in which you're rigid like a soldier. If you're used to deep breathing, your body will naturally want to correct a posture when it's not right.

Straighten your back, relax your shoulders and neck, and lift up and open your chest. Stick out your butt a little bit in the back and straighten your hips. Pull your chin in slightly. You'll find that if you pull your heavy head up, it will find a stable position right up on the spine.

Bad posture is when your back is hunched and your chest dropped, your shoulders and hips aren't level, and parts of your organs are suppressed. When your breath is shallow, even a bad posture may feel alright.

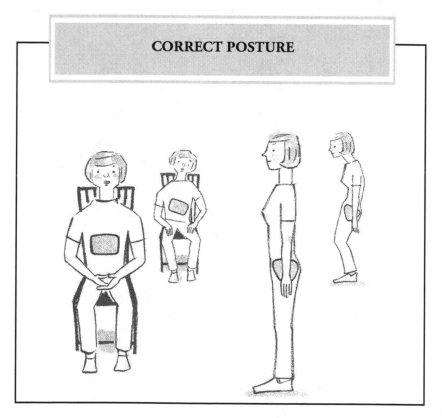

CORRECT POSTURE

LEARN CORRECT BREATHING TECHNIQUES 4
Balancing Inhaling, Holding, and Exhaling

PERFECT BREATH TECHNIQUE

The word "Perfect" in Perfect Breath Technique means that this technique perfectly brings out one's natural breathing ability. It also indicates a breath that sends the air to the lungs completely, in which the time devoted to inhaling, holding, and exhaling are in a perfect proportion to absorb air and *Ki* without waste.

The key is to move the diaphragm well, to expand and contract the respiratory system muscles in the chest and the back, and to fill all the spaces, such as those in the lungs and thoracic cavity, with air. Even if you can't do this right away, you can learn to control the rhythm of inhaling, holding, and exhaling in order to inhale and exhale air and *Ki* most effectively. You will get closer to perfect breath by letting go of physical and mental tension. The closer your natural unconscious breath is to perfect breath, the more stable your body and mind will be.

Inhalation

1. Breathe out first and then carefully breathe in by relaxing your tightened abdomen and expanding your lower abdomen, which lowers your diaphragm. In the beginning, your upper stomach area may expand, but as you get used to this exercise, you will be able to expand your lower abdomen.

2. Keep inhaling as if you're opening up your chest or lower ribs to the side, and your expanded lower abdomen will shrink a little. Continue inhaling to open your chest and the middle ribs, front and back. Continue inhaling to lift your chest and ribs up, breathing until the air reaches below the collarbones. This will totally fill your lungs.

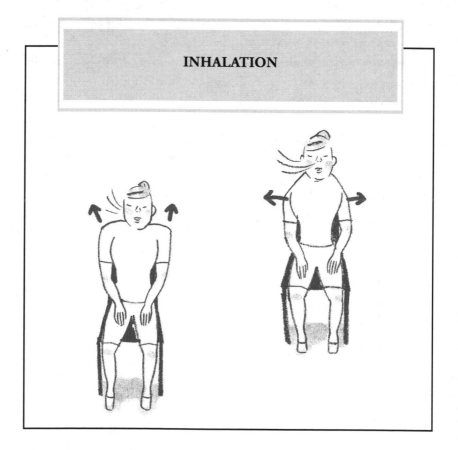

INHALATION

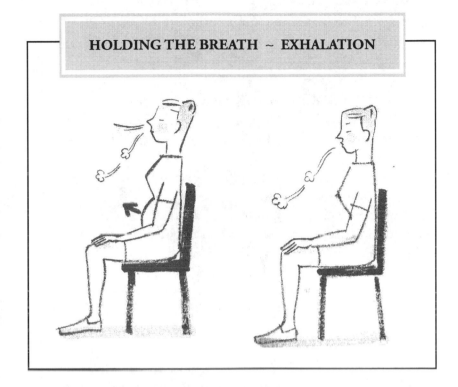

Holding the Breath

If you let out a little bit of the air you inhaled, your diaphragm will drop down and your abdomen will expand again. Tighten your anus, push the air into your stomach, and hold. Let go about 10 to 15 percent of the air that you inhaled.

Exhalation

Pull back on the force you used to hold the breath, and start exhaling carefully, not letting the air out at once but steadily controlling the amount of the air you breathe out. If you find it difficult to let the air out naturally after you exhale a certain amount, you may need to squeeze the air out intentionally by tightening and pushing the abdomen toward spine. After you've exhaled 80 to 90 percent of the air, your body will naturally begin to inhale just by the act of your letting go of the force to tighten your abdomen and straighten your spine.

LEARN CORRECT BREATHING TECHNIQUES 5
OPENING THE PATH OF KI

CLEANSING BREATHING TECHNIQUE (BASIC)

This is another very important technique, which can direct *Ki,* open the path of *Ki,* and cleanse *Ki.* If you think breathing techniques are only about breathing air in and out, this technique will open your eyes.

When I was still a beginning yoga student, my nerves were very tense and I was exhausted, but I was surprised to find that ten minutes of Cleansing Breathing Exercise eliminated my tiredness like magic. I was also successful in managing a severe toothache for half a day by practicing this technique for ten minutes.

The basis of this exercise is very similar to the Perfect Breathing Technique. If you're able to master directing *Ki* with your imagination, this can be very helpful in your daily life. This exercise can be done anytime, anywhere, and can be applied in many ways.

Inhalation

Breathe in and imagine that fresh air, oxygen, and *Ki* energy are slowly entering your body, making you feel good and healing you. You feel healed and good.

Holding

Hold the breath and imagine that concentrated energy is spreading throughout your entire body and that your cells are becoming rejuvenated and active.

Exhalation

Purse your lips and imagine that *Jaki,* or negative energy, is leaving through your lips. Because better visualization results in a better effect, divide your breath into three parts so you can be more strongly focused.

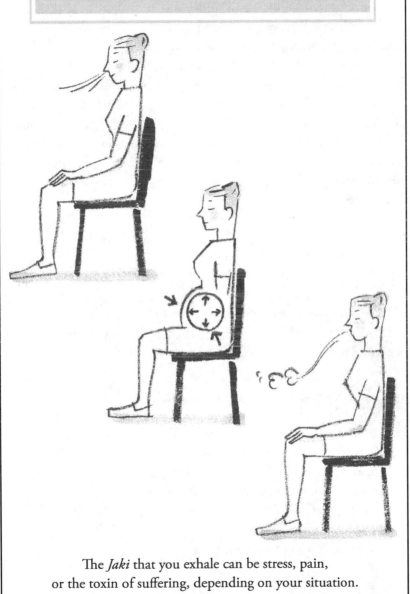

TECHNIQUES OPENING THE PATH OF *KI*:
CLEANSING BREATHING TECHNIQUE (BASIC)

The *Jaki* that you exhale can be stress, pain,
or the toxin of suffering, depending on your situation.

TANDEN BREATHING TECHNIQUE

I think *Tanden* is the greatest wisdom of the body ever discovered in the East. Those who discovered this and named it *Tanden* realized that collecting *Ki* into the place below the belly button, deep inside of the body, stabilizes our body physiologically and energetically. Indian yoga tradition has a similar idea, called *Uddiyana*, which means the throne of god. *Tanden* (*Tan Tien* in Chinese pronunciation) is a Chinese Taoist word; *"Tan"* meaning ageless longevity, and *"Den"* means a place to cultivate *Tan*. In Japan, we also call *Tanden* *"Hara,"* a word that is used to indicate *Tanden* even in America as well.

The *Tanden* Breathing Technique was developed by devising breathing methods to gather *Ki* in *Tanden*. There are some differences in the styles developed by different people, but they are all an application of abdominal breathing. Your life force will become vigorous if you cultivate *Tanden*.

I will now introduce a method to gather force in *Tanden* by doing abdominal breathing and creating pressure in the abdominal area when you exhale. If you do this several times, you will feel your *Tanden* being filled up.

1. Exhale completely and lean the upper body slightly forward. Relax your solar plexus and do abdominal breathing, expanding the lower belly first. *Ki* can't travel down enough if the stomach or upper abdomen is expanded; therefore, try to expand your lower abdomen first and then move upward, as if your belly button is facing up.

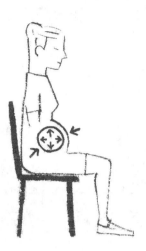

2. As in Perfect Breathing Technique (p.??), if you keep inhaling, your chest opens up and your lower belly shrinks. When you've breathed in about 80 percent of your capacity, let the air out through your nose slightly to relax your chest, then concentrate the air in the abdomen and tighten your anus as you hold your breath. Your lower abdomen will feel like a balloon. As you do this, imagine that your Tanden is charged with energy and warming up. Each time you hold the breath, your Tanden becomes fuller.

3. When you exhale, don't relax. Push *Ki* into the abdomen, tightening your anus and lower belly at the same time. Breathe out as you balance the force in these three different parts. Your lower belly will sink as you keep exhaling. Tighten your lower belly and hold when you have exhaled about 90 percent of the air. Then relax your tightened lower belly and go back to inhaling, as you did in step one.

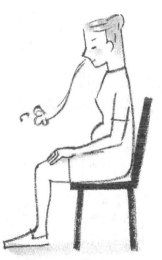

Begin inhaling, holding, and exhaling in a 1:1:1 ratio, then stretch it out to 1:2:2. If possible, holding can be extended to 4.
It's unnecessary to do more. For example, inhale for 6 counts, hold for 12 counts, and exhale for 12 counts, repeating this six times.

LEARN CORRECT BREATHING TECHNIQUES 7
COLLECT *KI* IN *TANDEN*

SHIKOFUMI, THE SPINE TWISTING BREATHING TECHNIQUE

Shikofumi, from our traditional sport, Sumo, is actually a wonderful breathing technique. On the physical level, it strengthens your legs and lower back, but it also energetically eliminates the tension in the upper body and concentrates *Ki* in *Tanden*. By lowering *Ki* to *Tanden*, Sumo wrestlers let go of anxiety so that they can be calm enough for their match. If they didn't do *Shikofumi,* not only would they have more injuries, but the matches would be more aggressive and less dignified. Spine Twisting Technique in this position lets *Ki* in through the spine, so it is very effective.

1. Keep your legs wide apart. Holding your knees with both hands, breathe in, shifting your weight to your left leg, and lift up your right leg.

2. Breathe out about half of the air and forcefully put your right foot down on the ffoor, holding and pushing the breath into your lower abdomen with a "hm" sound. Hold your breath for a moment. Keeping your hands on your knees, lower your anus and exhale the rest of the air. Try to lower your butt as much as you can so that the bottoms of your thighs form a parallel line, or an M-shaped line, to the ffoor.

3. Inhale in this position, exhale as you push your right shoulder out and twist your upper body, and inhale. Push your knees with your hands and stretch out your spine.

* Repeat several times on both sides.

COLLECT *KI* IN *TANDEN*

PRACTICAL BREATHING TECHNIQUES

"I'm always busy with work, study, and housework."

"I have problems with relationships."

"I'm worried about my health"

Our modern lifestyle seems to be very stressful and exhausting. The best way to handle this is to rest and refresh, but people rarely have enough time. They carry the stress and tiredness with them and create a bad spiral, building up more stress and strain. I think many people are like that.

If you're one of them, I'd like you to master the breathing techniques I'm going to introduce here. These are techniques that can help you control your mind, balance your body, or enhance your relationships. I always emphasize that the right way to practice breathing techniques is to apply the proper technique to each situation in your daily life in order to better manage yourself. When you change a negative situation to a positive one, you enhance a situation that didn't allow your mind and body to find balance. In order to do this, you need to observe your breath and posture in the negative situation and create the opposite.

For example, when you're stressed out, your neck tenses up, your energy rises, and your breath becomes short and loud. You can balance this by intentionally creating the opposite breathing and posture. In this case, you relax your neck and take a long slow breath. Somehow, you feel less stressed out.

To master controlling yourself with breathing techniques, you first need to be aware of and sensitive to the relationship between breath and posture, mind and body, and emotion and desire. It's important that you practice different breathing techniques so that you know what kind of effects they have.

Please learn the following techniques well so that you can apply them when necessary.

1. WHEN YOUR ENTIRE BODY IS EXHAUSTED

1. When you inhale, imagine that fresh air is flowing in, washing away the tiredness and refreshing you.

2. Hold your breath and visualize gathering all the stressful elements in your mouth.

3. Purse your lips and exhale with the sound "phew," letting out about one-third of the air in the lungs, along with all the stressful elements.

4. Stop exhaling and visualize just as you did in step two. Exhale another one-third of the air, then repeat the visualization and exhale the rest of the air.

Do this about ten times, then go back to your natural breath.

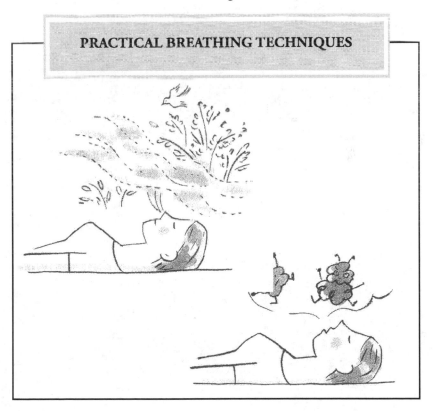

PRACTICAL BREATHING TECHNIQUES

2. WHEN YOU HAVE PAIN IN YOUR BODY
《SUCH AS A TOOTHACHE》

1. As you inhale, bring your attention to where the pain is, imagining that you are inhaling through this area and that fresh healing *Ki* is being drawn to the pain and curing it. *Although the air comes in through your nose, it's important to imagine that the healing *Ki* is entering directly where the pain is.

2. Hold your breath and imagine that you are gathering all the elements of pain to the tip of your mouth.

3. Purse your lips and slowly exhale the elements of pain along with one-third of the air, making the sound "phew."

4. Stop exhaling for a moment and repeat step two, exhaling another one-third of the air in the lungs. Stop once again and repeat, exhaling the last third.

Do this about ten times, then go back to your natural breath.

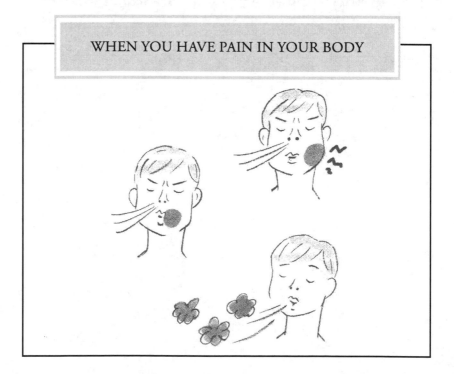

WHEN YOU HAVE PAIN IN YOUR BODY

3. WHEN YOU HAVE SPECIFIC PROBLEMS
ﬁSUCH AS IN THE STOMACH, LIVER, INTESTINES, UTERUS, ETC.ﬁ

1. As you breathe in, bring your attention to the diseased part of your body and imagine that you are breathing in through that part. Imagine that healing energy is drawn to this part, healing and energizing the cells. The cells are healed and energized.

2. Hold your breath for a moment and imagine that toxic elements of the disease are gathered at the tip of your mouth.

3. Purse your lips and slowly release the toxic elements along with one-third of the air, making the sound "phew."

4. Stop exhaling and repeat the visualization in step two, breathing out another one-third of the air in the lungs in the same manner. Stop once again and repeat step two, exhaling completely. * Do this about ten times, then go back to your normal breath.

4. TO LOWER KI WHEN YOU'RE NERVOUS OR ANXIOUS

When you're nervous or anxious, you subconsciously inhale forcefully and your shoulders, neck, and hands are tense. If you find yourself in such a situation, you should intentionally do the opposite.

1. Exhale and shake your upper body to relax. Open your legs and place your hands on the knees in *Shikofumi* posture, lowering your hips several times as you exhale.

2. As you exhale, say *"Yoisho"* and do *Shiko* several times. Alternatively, squat about ten times.

3. If you follow this with deep relaxing breaths, your nervous tension will disappear and you'll feel calmer.

*If you have difficulty doing Shiko or squatting, you can get a similar effect by tightening your anus as you exhale slowly and relaxing it as you inhale.

TO LOWER KI WHEN YOU'RE
NERVOUS OR ANXIOUS

TO RECOVER FROM SHOCK QUICKLY

5. TO RECOVER FROM SHOCK QUICKLY

When someone is taken by surprise, they stop breathing after the quick inhalation, their pinky toe tightens, and their big toe points into the air. They usually recover by exhaling on a sigh or saying something like "You surprised me!" But if their chest is still tight and their exhalation is forceless, they remain in shock.

1. To quickly recover from surprise, circle your arms wide and take deep breaths.

2. Do *Shikofumi* several times, trying to grab the floor with the big toes and heels, and putting force into the arch of your feet several times as you exhale.

*If you have difficulty doing *Shiko*, you can get a similar effect by tightening your anus as you exhale slowly and relaxing it as you inhale.

6. TO OVERCOME FEAR

When someone is scared, they tend to breathe in strongly and all of a sudden. Their upper body tenses up, and their legs and lower back weaken. Then their upper body starts to shiver or their knees start to tremble. In the worst cases, after tremendous tension, they may subconsciously let go of tension in the eliminative organs, resulting in incontinence.

1. First, try to laugh "ha ha ha" in order to relax, loosen, and expand the contraction and tension in your body and regain strength in your legs and hips.

2. Forcefully shake your upper body, circle your arms, hold your hands, and turn the arms over and stretch them out over your head to let go of nervousness.

3. Place your palms on the wall, stretching the back of your thighs and Achilles tendons. Alternatively, do *Shikofumi* with strength in your feet, or exhale slowly as you tighten your anus and inhale as you relax it.

ノ✓

7. TO ENHANCE CONCENTRATION

In the martial arts, such as kendo, if the ability of both players is about the same, it's likely that the one with less focused mind will lose the match. One tends to lose focus and become unguarded when they're about to breathe in, and that's when the opponent attacks. In order to make it difficult for your opponent to read your breathing, you need to use a long, quiet breath in which you don't seem to be breathing at all. In other words, you shouldn't consciously hold your breath, but focus as you exhale slowly, and breathe slowly and quietly as you breathe in.

Unfortunately, no breathing technique will boost someone's ability to concentrate right away if they're not good at concentrating. The best you can do is to enhance your breath by engaging in each action without mind chattering.

Another way to enhance concentration is to become accustomed to stretching your whole body, including the chest, neck, hips, and shoulders, as shown on the next page. When your body is stiff or distorted, stimulation in the inner body can cause stress, which distracts you when you want to concentrate.

When you move your body, consciously try to align your breath with your movements. For example, when you walk, align your breath with your steps in a "breathe out, out, in, in" rhythm, or when you cook, align your breath with the movements of the knife you're using. You can do this in sports too. For example, when you play golf, breathe in when you lift the golf club and breathe out as you swing it.

It may also help to tighten your anus as you breathe out slowly for eight counts, relaxing it as you breathe in for four counts, and repeating this three times. Do this many times throughout the day whenever you can. When your anus is tightened, your *Ki* doesn't get stuck in your head, and you have more clarity, which helps reduce mistakes.

I'd like you to also practice consciously some other things in your daily life: the Swinging Arms Breathing Technique, which balances the natural body to be **"upper body empty and lower body full"** and is a foundation for concentration; and the Counting Breathing Technique, which cultivates concentration by focusing on your natural breath.

Stretch everyday and balance your body.

1. Bend your upper body forward as you exhale. Come back up as you inhale. Bend backward as you exhale. Repeat these motions.

2. Rotate your hip as you exhale. Do this eight times on each side.

3. Interlace your fingers in the back, turning your palms out as you exhale and pushing out your chest. Inhale and relax your chest and hands, and repeat.

SWINGING ARMS BREATHING TECHNIQUE

Keep your feet wider than your hips, with your little toes parallel and your arms hanging loose. Turn your upper body to the side so that your arms naturally hit your body without forcing them.

Count one each time you turn. Count two, three, four as you exhale; and inhale as you count five, six. The exhalation should be two times longer than the inhalation.

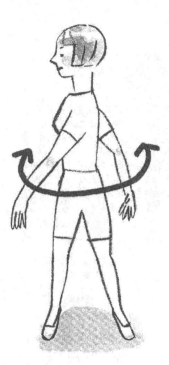

COUNTING BREATHING TECHNIQUE

Observe your breath: When you breathe in, your chest and stomach expand, and when you breathe out, your chest and stomach shrink. As you observe, count each breath one, two, three... When you count ten, go back to one. Get used to practicing this about ten minutes a day.

8. TO BE MORE PASSIONATE

If you don't have energy and are apathetic in everything, your lower back will be stiff, your neck will be weak, your chest will drop, and your chin will stick out.

You also sigh more, lack energy, and your breath is short and shallow.

When you find yourself like this, stick out your chest and take some deep breaths. Then bend forward as you exhale in order to stretch your back.

Inhale, energizing your stomach, and bring in *Ki* by force. Then hold your breath (called *Kumbak* in yoga, as previously described).

After this, practice the Strengthening *Ki* Breathing Technique and Chest Banging Breathing Technique. The instructions follow.

STRENGTHENING KI BREATHING TECHNIQUE

1. Make loose fists, bending your elbows 90 degrees and placing them by your sides, and breathe in deeply.

2. Forcefully push your arm out in front of you as you exhale on "khaaaa." Repeat this motion quickly, three or four times a second. Do this until you exhale all the air, then stop, take a deep breath, and breathe naturally several times. Repeat the push-out. This will cause your body temperature to rise.

STRENGTHENING *KI* BREATHING TECHNIQUE

CHEST BANGING
BREATHING TECHNIQUE

In this technique, you imitate the movement of a gorilla threatening others. Breathe in deeply and hold your breath as you push your chest out. Then make loose fists and bang your chest at least ten times as you breathe out with a "wooooo" sound, like a dog growling. Breathe once to rest and repeat the process.

9. TO EASE NERVOUSNESS

If you observe yourself when you're nervous, you'll realize that your solar plexus and neck are stiff and your breath is fast, short, and aggressive. You may also close your mouth tight or have a stiff face.

If this becomes habitual, your abdomen loses its softness and your navel tightens. This can make it difficult for you to relax, and make you tired and sick.

Remember, being nervous or upset is a stupid thing that only hurts you.

When you find yourself in a situation like this, the Solar Plexus Stretch Breathing Technique and L-Shaped Relaxing Breathing Technique are most effective.

If you can't do these exercises (for example, when you're driving), do abdominal breathing, tightening your anus as you breathe out. These will be most effective if you intentionally smile as you do them, because sometimes facial tension stimulates the brain and makes you anxious.

SOLAR PLEXUS STRETCH BREATHING TECHNIQUE

To eliminate nervousness, you need to relax your stiff solar plexus. Place the index, middle, and ring fingers of both hands on your solar plexus, massaging your solar plexus with them as you slowly breathe out and bend forward. Then bring your upper body up and do the same thing as you exhale and bend forward. If you practice this for five or six times, your solar plexus will become softer.

L-SHAPED RELAXING BREATHING TECHNIQUE

The purpose of this exercise is to loosen your neck and chest. Lift your arms in an L-shape and open your chest as you breathe in. Try to squeeze your shoulder blades together and let them go as you breathe out. Repeat this several times. Then take some deep breaths, rotating your neck.

10. TO CONTROL YOUR ANGER

When your nervousness becomes more aggressive, your shoulders tense up and your back becomes stiff. I've seen drawings of an angry person with his hair standing on end. When you're angry, your center rises to your head and your scalp is tensed as well. Anger comes from our instinct to protect ourselves. It enables us to fight against enemies by making the most of our abilities. Animals can discharge this anger when it's no longer necessary, but humans hold onto the anger, and even remember it much later on.

We need to handle our anger well, to understanding that anger is toxic to our bodies and minds. It raises blood pressure and damages the heart. But it's also important that we not withhold our anger, because un-released toxic energy damages the liver, which can be quite dangerous.

LAUGHING BREATHING AND STRETCHING BREATHING

Laughing Breathing is the most effective breath for easing anger. Take a deep breath and stretch as you breathe out, leaning back and rotating your neck in order to release the tension from your upper body and back.

LAUGHING BREATHING AND STRETCHING BREATHING

SQUAT BREATHING TECHNIQUE

Keep your feet shoulder-width apart and, as you breathe in, squat without leaning forward, with your hands on your head and your chest open. As you breathe out, stand on your big toes and push the ffoor. This will be most effective if you breathe out forcefully and tighten or push in your abdomen. Do this about ten times to lower the *Ki* that's in the head. Also helpful are the Anus Tightening Breathing Technique (p.32), *Shikofumi* (p.100), and Back Thigh Stretching (p.120).

Finally, breathe out the toxin of anger with the Cleansing Breathing Technique. Close your eyes gently, imagining that you're breathing in refreshing, clean *Ki*. Gather the remaining toxins from all around your body into your mouth, and purse your lips as you exhale the toxins along with the air. Do this for a few minutes.

SQUAT BREATHING TECHNIQUE

11. TO RESOLVE INSOMNIA

Everyone has had the experience of being unable to fall asleep at night even though they're tired because they can't stop thinking about something they're really concerned about. Even if you could fall asleep with sleeping pills, that wouldn't solve the fundamental problem.

If a doctor diagnoses you with "insomnia," you might assume you have a disease, but it's just that you can't sleep when you want to. If you use your body until you're exhausted, you'll fall asleep easily.

It's not easy to fall asleep right away when you've been nervous, even if you're tired. That's because an unbalanced stimulus of distress is preventing you from falling asleep.

There are two kinds of distress: partial and whole body. When you're partially distressed, you lack energy in certain places, but not in other parts of your body. In this situation, it's best to find balance by releasing the remaining energy through exercise rather than rest.

When you can't sleep, your energy tends to be stuck in your shoulders, neck, and head, and your Achilles tendons are contracted.

Therefore, you need to stretch the muscles in the back of the legs, one leg at a time. You may use a towel to do it. Then bend forward, not to a point that's painful, and take about ten deep breaths with a smile on your face.

Next, lie on your stomach with your palms by the side of your chest and take deep breaths as you arch your back. If you slowly rotate your shoulders and neck, your *Ki* and blood will move down to your torso, eliminating the blockages in your head and making it easier to fall asleep.

The tension you feel when you've been using your head to concentrate is a typical nervous—not physical—distress. In this situation, swing your upper body with your arms hanging as you take deep breaths (p.112), or go for a walk and try to align your breath with your movements.

Alternatively, you can stretch your back or the back of your legs using a tree in your backyard. Touching trees is recommended as well. If it is too late at night, use an object in your room to stretch against.

Stretching the Back of Your Legs with Deep Breaths

Arching Your Back with Deep Breaths

Stretching Your Back and the Back of Your Legs as You Exhale, Using a Tree

12. BREATHING TECHNIQUES FOR WALKING AND JOGGING

Consciously align your movements with the rhythm of your breath, aware that by walking or running you're practicing breathing. Basically, you inhale, inhale, exhale, exhale… and align the movements of your hands and feet with your breath. Try to put more force on the exhalation than on the inhalation.

When you walk, land with your heel first and push the ground with your first and second toes. Bring your awareness to the bottoms of your feet as you land with your heel, and then lift your heel up, along with the first and second toes.

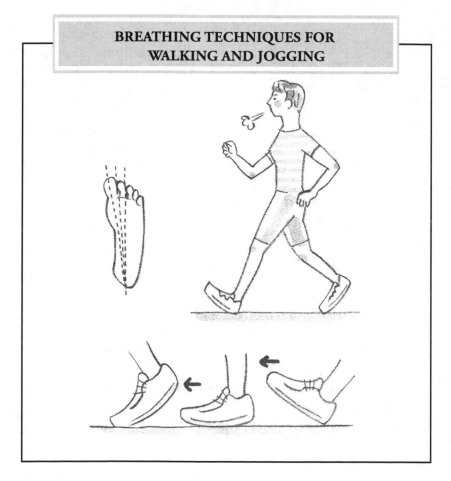

BREATHING TECHNIQUES FOR
WALKING AND JOGGING

13. TO PROMOTE ELIMINATION AND
SOLVE CONSTIPATION

People who are constipated even though they get plenty of fiber seem to breathe very weakly and speak very quietly. On the other hand, people with loud voices who are able to greatly contract and expand their respiratory organs are less likely to be constipated. In yoga we teach that the power of elimination is in proportion to the power of breath. There's a reason for this. We naturally exercise our stomach as we breathe, and its stimulation promotes peristaltic movement in the intestines. If your breath is weak, it can't support peristaltic movement.

We tend to hold our breath as we exert ourselves when we relieve our bowels. But this raises the blood pressure too quickly and damages the anus. Therefore, try a posture and breathing that promote peristaltic movement naturally. When you sit on the toilet, straighten your spine and relax your body, breathing out slowly through an open mouth as you tighten your stomach. This is even more effective if you push your stomach with your hands as you exhale.

If you have problems with constipation, try practicing the Abdominal Breathing Technique (p.90), which strengthens the stomach. Regularly practice the basic training—in which you exhale and tighten your abdomen, let go and let your stomach expand naturally to inhale, and then intentionally inhale more.

Some techniques can be practiced in bed. With one knee or both knees bent, breathe out, keeping your palms together. Then turn the palms over and stretch your arms above your head. Relax as you breathe in and stretch again as you breathe out. Repeat this about sixteen times. Then pull one knee or both knees to your chest with your hands and take about sixteen deep breaths. You can practice this when you wake up in the morning or before you go to sleep at night.

The *Tanden* Breathing Technique (p.98) is effective as well. You could also try taking deep breaths as you push the acupuncture point called *Gokoku*, or lightly smack the top of your head with your fist in a clockwise motion around the point called *Hyakkei*, which is located where the line of the nose and the lines from both ears meet.

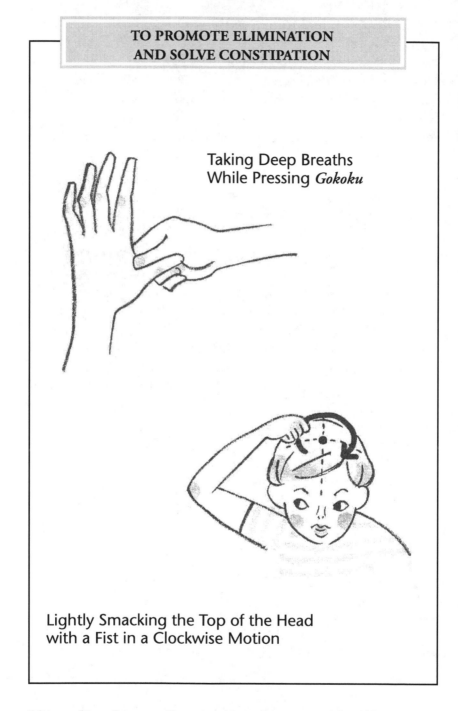

Taking Deep Breaths
While Pressing *Gokoku*

Lightly Smacking the Top of the Head
with a Fist in a Clockwise Motion

Breathing Techniques
That Can Be Practiced in
Bed

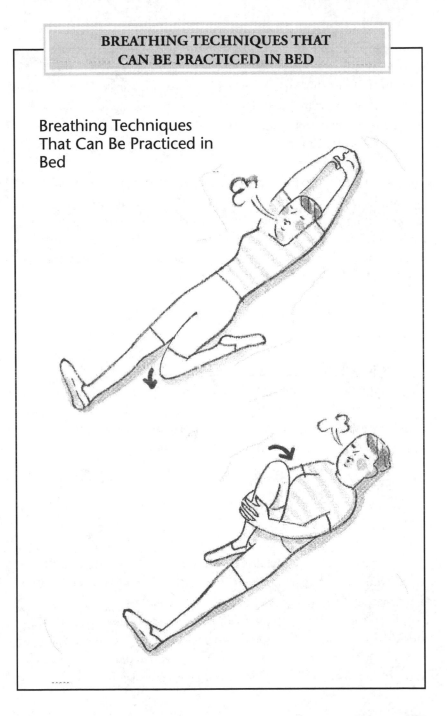

14. TO ELIMINATE EYESTRAIN

More people than ever work with computers all day, and many of them are troubled by tiredness and dryness in the eyes. In the past, they could have looked out the window to see green nature and to have a healing moment, even at work. But today, all we see in the city are artificial colors and lights such as traffic lights, street signs, billboards, advertisements, the shine of metal, and buildings. Our eyes are even more strained by these unnatural stimuli.

Why do our eyes get tired? Let's use the arms as an example.

Which makes you more tired: hammering a nail above your head or one below your heart? You get more tired when you hammer a nail above your head, and your arms and shoulders become tired too. That's because when there's less blood flow, nutrients can't be transported and waste matter builds up. You get tired in a different way when you use your arms without straining than when you strain them. When your arms are tired, you can quickly eliminate the tiredness by loosening the muscles through massage or stretching, or by warming them to promote blood circulation.

It's the same with the eyes. One reason our eyes get tired is that tensing the muscles around the eyes causes bad blood circulation. When you use your eyes, it's important to avoid tensing them. For example, you could try looking at your computer screen with a smile, as if you were looking at a baby instead of staring at the computer. That way, even if you look at the computer for the same length of time, your eyes won't get as tired. The key to not getting tired is to relax and enjoy whatever you do.

It's also important to relax your muscles after you use your eyes for a long time. Tools last a long time if you take good care of them. So do eyes. I will now introduce four effective techniques for treating the eyes: Eight-Direction Stretch Breathing Technique, Perspective Stretch Breathing Technique, Eye Pressure Point Stimulation Technique, and Hand *Ki* Illumination Technique.

Tiredness of the eyes comes from stiffness in the muscles around them. If you look far into the distance or exercise your eyes, the blood will flow more easily, eliminating stiffness. If you're tense, the blood flow is constricted, so the key is to relax and let go of tension.

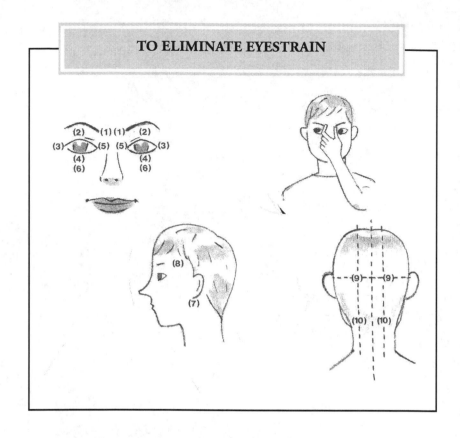

Eight-Direction Stretch Breathing Technique

1. Move your eyeball up as you exhale. Keep looking up for several seconds, then let it go and bring it back to the center. Take a breath and go on to the next step.

2. Do the same thing in the following directions: down, up right, down left, right, left, down right, up left. * When you're finished, reverse the directions and do the exercise the other way around.

* Do this with your face straight forward.

Perspective Stretch Breathing Technique

1. Breathe in and slowly breathe out as you look at a point, such as a tree in the far distance. Relax and keep watching for ten to twenty

seconds, with a smile on your face. Then blink your eyes several times to loosen the tension.

2. Place your palm about one foot from your eyes and watch the lines of the palm for about ten to twenty seconds in a relaxed state.

3. Close your eyes gently and rest them for ten to twenty seconds.
* Repeat this several times.

Eye Pressure Point Stimulation Technique

1. Massage the points next to the eyebrows with your thumb and index finger.

2. Press the points above the eyelids with your thumbs as if you were pushing them up.

3. Press the sides of your eyes with your index fingers from inside to outside.

4. Press the points below your eyes with index fingers as if you were pulling them down.

5. Massage the tear duct with your thumbs and index fingers as if you were picking them up.

6. Place your index fingers about an inch outside of the nostrils and press the points toward the eyes.

7. Place your thumbs below your ears, with the other four fingers supporting the head, and press the points toward the eyes.

8. Place your thumbs on your temples, with the other four fingers supporting the head, and press the points toward the eyes, rotating.

9. Place your thumbs on your head directly in back of your eyes, with the other four fingers supporting the head, and press the points toward the eyes.

10. Place your thumbs on the points at the bottom of the skull, at the outside corners of the indentation of the neck, with the other four fingers supporting the head, and press them toward the eyes.
*Stimulate the ten points ten times each as you exhale.

HAND KI ILLUMINATION TECHNIQUE
APPLICATION OF CLEANSING BREATH TECHNIQUE.

Put your hands on your eyes to supply *Ki* and release tiredness and unwanted matter.

1. Massage your palms to warm them up.

2. Cupping your hands, place them so that the centers of your palms are right over your eyes. Your eyes should be closed. Slowly breathe in, imagining that the eyes are absorbing *Ki* from the hands.

3. Hold your breath for a few seconds and bring your awareness to your mouth, gathering all the tiredness of your eyes into your mouth. Purse your lips and slowly exhale the tiredness and unwanted matter from your eyes. Don't exhale all at once, but rather in two or three stages.

* Repeat this about ten times to brighten your vision and eliminate tiredness.

*Note: In order for you to see how you should breathe, the illustration shows only one hand.

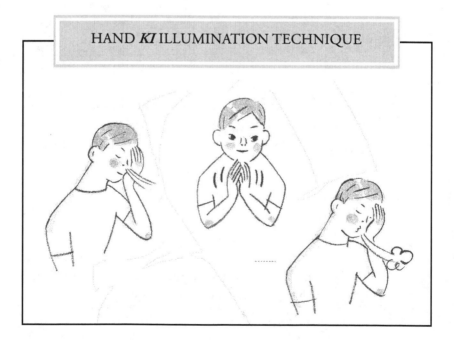

HAND *KI* ILLUMINATION TECHNIQUE

15. TO PREVENT A HANGOVER

Sit comfortably or lie down and close your eyes gently. Breathe in as slowly and deeply as you can, imagining very fresh air coming in as you breathe.

Imagine that you are gathering the alcohol in your body and concentrating it into your mouth. Purse your lips and let it out. You can make this exercise more effective by imagining that you are spitting out and burning the alcohol in your body, just like a circus performer spits out oil to light a fire.

* Doing this after you've had too many drinks can help you feel better and prevent a hangover. It can also be helpful when you are hung over the next morning.

TO PREVENT A HANGOVER

16. TO CONTROL YOUR APPETITE

You can control your appetite to prevent obesity and related problems with this technique to manage hunger, even if you don't eat or eat very little.

1. Sit relaxed with your back straight and your eyes closed. Breathe in with your lips pursed as if drinking juice through a straw and imagine that you're consuming soup full of nutrition. Breathe abdominally so that your stomach expands as you do this.

2. Once you've finished inhaling, hold your breath and imagine that nutrition and *Ki* are spreading throughout your entire body, making the cells more alive.

3. Exhale slowly through your nose. Imagine that what's left of the nutrition you have absorbed is exiting with the air.

* Start with this proportion: inhale 1, hold 1, exhale 1, gradually extending to inhale 1, hold 2, exhale 1.

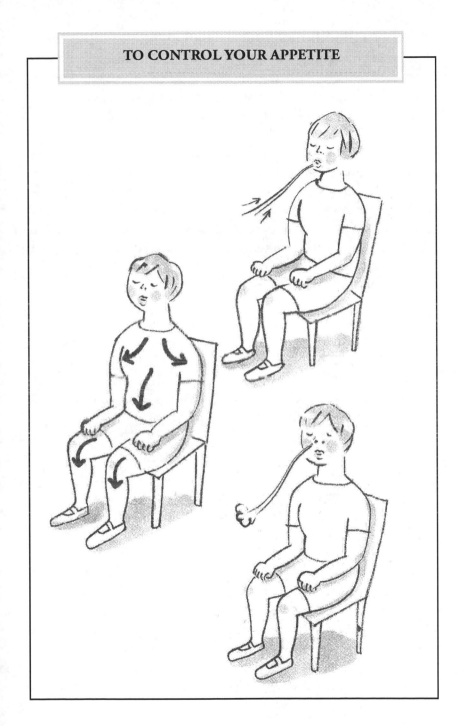

17. TO QUIT SMOKING SUCCESSFULLY

When you're trying to quit smoking, it's important to understand that by smoking you were trying to dissolve anxiety, stress, and nervousness. You won't be very successful if you try to quit smoking just because smoking is bad for your health. There are even those who have suffered from ulcerative colitis by trying to quit smoking. You need to rethink your work and the relationships that cause you so much stress leading to smoke, and find a way of thinking, working, and dealing with other people that stress you.

It's difficult to quit smoking successfully through intentions and techniques alone. You may sometimes find yourself unintentionally holding your breath when you're consumed by work. You take a cigarette break to change this type of breathing pattern. You might want to smoke after a meal in order to breathe, because you didn't taste or enjoy the food, or because your organs are strained.

Look at how you breathe when you smoke. You breathe in forcefully and breathe out slowly through your mouth.

In other words, you're practicing a breathing technique using smoke and nicotine tar.

Nicotine tar is harmful of course. It could be said that you neutralize your stress by taking in toxic matter in order to bring out your ability to balance the toxins in your body.

If you practice a breathing technique to help you quit smoking, your breath will at least be stable, and it could reduce your desire to smoke. You'll also realize how tasty the air really is, and might become disgusted by smoke.

If you are able to change your mindset about work, you will be even more successful at quitting smoking.

Sit comfortably and arch your back slightly. Breathe out through your mouth, making a "hoooo" sound as if breathing out the stress in your body. Pucker your lips as you do when you smoke, and inhale slowly for seven or eight seconds, imagining that fresh oxygen is neutralizing and purifying the toxic stress. Breathe deep into your body.

Keeping your lips in the same position, exhale with a "hooo" sound, imagining that you're letting go of stress. Imagine that you become more refreshed each time you breathe.

* Inhale and exhale in the proportion 1:1.
Repeat at least ten times whenever you feel like smoking.

18. TO MAINTAIN NORMAL BLOOD PRESSURE

High blood pressure, hyperlipemia, hyperglycosuria, and arteriosclerosis must be treated as soon as possible holistically through the mind, diet, breath, and exercise, because they can develop into heart disease or stroke.

High blood pressure is a state in which your heart pumps the blood out forcefully, because for some reason the blood won't flow well without high pressure. When there is insufficient blood circulation, particularly when the blood vessels of the internal organs are clogged, the cells of the organs can't take in enough oxygen. As a result, the cells have a shorter life span, which leads to decay of the organs and to aging of the entire body.

These symptoms are usually hardly recognizable because they're not accompanied by pain. Therefore, by the time you realize something is wrong you may have a serious problem.

One reason for bad blood circulation is that the blood becomes too thick and sticky to flow. In order to make the blood thinner, you need to change your diet. But you can also help by taking in more oxygen through deep breathing.

Another reason for bad blood circulation is that the blood vessels become stiff or narrow. This is brought on by a high-cholesterol diet, which causes arteriosclerosis.

Blood vessels are not just pipes that transport blood; they also function like muscles. Your blood pressure increases when you're angry or excited because not only the surrounding muscles but also the blood vessels themselves shrink.

It's important to keep your blood vessels healthy, along with the entire muscle system, in order to maintain your blood pressure at the appropriate level.

I'd like to introduce breathing techniques in three consecutive movements (A, B, and C).

Exercise A stretches the back of the legs, makes the shoulder-blade area flexible, expanding the respiratory muscles of the chest and back, and enhancing and balancing your breathing. Exercise B promotes the contraction and expansion ability of the respiratory muscles on the sides.

Exercise C gives you emotional stability, stimulats the balancing ability of the autonomic nerves, and helps control blood pressure.

    * Practice A to C consecutively.

EXERCISE A: TO STRETCH THE BACK OF THE LEGS AND EXPAND THE RESPIRATORY MUSCLES ON THE CHEST

1. Interlace your fingers on your back, turn the palms around, and breathe in.

2. As you breathe out, keep your back straight and bend forward until it is parallel to the ffoor, stretching the back of you legs.

3. Stand up as you inhale, and put your hands on your hips. As you exhale, arch your back slightly and come back to center. Bring your hands in front as you inhale.

* Repeat steps one through four at least four times.

EXERCISE A

EXERCISE B: TO STRETCH THE RESPIRATORY MUSCLES AT THE SIDE OF THE RIBS

1. Interlace your fingers in front of your abdomen and lift them up to your chest as you breathe in. Turn your palms up and lift your hands as you breathe out.

2. Bend your upper body to the left as you breathe in, and come back to center as you breathe out. Repeat on the right, opening your arms and bringing them down to your sides as you breathe in and come back to center.

* Repeat step two several times before bringing your hands down.

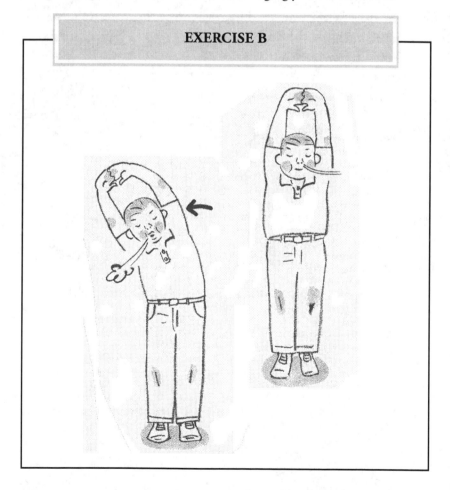

EXERCISE B

EXERCISE C: TO GATHER *KI* INTO THE ABDOMEN

1. Breathe in and lift your hands sideways above your head, the palms of your hands facing up.

2. Bring your hands down to the front with your fingertips meeting, and exhale completely.

   * Repeat steps one and two at least four times.

19. TO GAIN STAMINA

People who are always in high energy have stamina and endurance. When they project healthy energy, they gain more healthy energy, which gives them even more stamina.

Physical endurance depends on whether oxygen and nutrition spread well to the body's cells and whether metabolites and waste matters are properly eliminated. In other words, it depends on the quantity and quality of blood and its circulation. Physical training can enhance the ability of the cells to absorb oxygen, so appropriate physical exercise is essential if one's physical endurance is to be enhanced. Choose an exercise in which you can align your breath with your movements rhythmically, such as jogging, but try to emphasize the exhalation and don't waste energy unnecessarily.

Mental stamina has many aspects. One is that don't give up on things too easily, but continue patiently, with a faith that there will always be a way, even if you're stuck in a situation, or if you fall down along the way. The most important thing is to do everything without unnecessary tension or nervousness and to be focused on the "here and now." This isn't something you can acquire instantly through a breathing technique. It's a holistic ability, so you need to practice basic breathing techniques daily, such as Breathing Exercises, Perfect Breathing, *Tanden* Breathing, and Cleansing Breathing.

I'd like to introduce two breathing techniques to activate vital energy and strengthen physical endurance.

One is called the Bellows Breathing Technique, a very traditional yogic breathing method. It activates the autonomic nerves, and awakens and brings out the life force.

The other is called the Breath Held Jogging Breathing Technique. Marathon runners train in high altitudes, where the air is thin, because when we move our muscles in thin air, our body tries to adapt by enhancing the ability of the blood and cells so that they can absorb more oxygen. One reason that holding your breath is important in yoga practice is that it brings out our ability to adapt to a low-oxygen situation.

Bellows Breathing Technique

Sit on a chair and correct your posture. Close your mouth, touch your tongue to the roof of your mouth, and quickly breathe in and out through your nose like a bellows. Maintain a speed of three breaths per second as you repeatedly expand and contract your abdomen. When you've completed twenty breaths, return to normal breathing to rest for five or six breaths, then complete another twenty breaths. Increase the number to thirty and repeat the process three times once you're more comfortable with it.

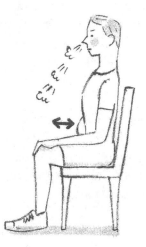

Breath-Held Jogging Breathing Technique

Begin breathing to the rhythm of your feet: inhale, inhale, exhale, exhale (inhale 1, exhale 1). Then begin to hold your breath as you get used to it: Inhale, inhale, hold, hold, exhale, exhale (inhale 1, hold 1, exhale 1). Then move on to inhale 1, hold 1, exhale 2; then inhale 1, hold 2, exhale 2. Try to work up to inhale 1, hold 4, exhale 2.

* Don't hold the breath longer or it will strain your body. Don't try too hard; adapt slowly to holding your breath for a longer time.

20. TO IMPROVE YOUR HEALTHY LIFE

Laughter leads your body and mind to a healthier state. It is scientifically proven that laughing makes immune-related blood cells such as NK cells and macrophages active and enhances immune power.

Use this breathing technique to make yourself laugh even though nothing is funny, or when you are sad, angry, struggling, or facing hardship. A breathing technique that imitates laughter can actually create laughter. Over the long term, there's a huge difference between someone who laughs once a day and someone who laughs only once a month. Laughing not only improves one's physical condition, it can also change relationships and increase luck. When you laugh you release positive energies and at the same time get happy *Ki* and energy from your surroundings.

If laughing feels like too much, try to smile. When you're smiling, your breath naturally becomes relaxed and soft. When your cheeks are lifted in the position of a smile, your memories of smiling activate and relax your brain.

The Laughter Breathing Technique (Vocalized and Non-vocalized) is done this way: Exhale completely. Holding your arms in the shape of a one, arch your back slightly as you inhale deeply. Imitate the way you breathe when you laugh out loud silently, exaggerating the breath. As you repeat this several times, you may begin to feel funny and start laughing out loud. If you don't want to surprise people by suddenly laughing out loud, you can do just the breath, without voice or movement, depending on your situation.

The Smiling Breathing Technique is done in front of a mirror. Close your eyes and imagine something that evokes a smile, such as a cute baby or an animal. Be aware of the muscles in your face. Then open your eyes and look at your face thoroughly in the mirror. Close your eyes again and try to remember the breath and the feeling, so that you can apply them when you're with other people.

Laughter Breathing Technique
(Vocalized and Non-vocalized)
⁁ Can be done standing up or sitting down.

Smiling Breathing Technique (with a Mirror)

21. TO BE SUCCESSFUL IN BUSINESS

Once you learn the key to controlling your breath, you will not only be able to control your desire, emotions, and mind, but also be able to read other people's breaths. In business, it is important to know what other people are thinking. If you can read other people's thoughts and feelings, you can manage to go with the flow, or even lead and guide others well.

To Read Other People's Breaths

In order to read other people's breaths, you need to clear and sharpen your senses. The Spine Shaking Breathing Technique on page 148 will train you to listen to your body. If you don't have time for this, spend five minutes or so practicing the "Free Rocking Breathing Technique," which is also effective.

You've probably had the experience of trying to force yourself to go a little farther back and forth on a swing. The Swinging Breathing Technique on page 212 is like this. You deepen your breath gradually. You also internally correct your posture while deepening your breath, so you can create a posture that matches the situation you're in or the person you're with.

Align Your Breath with the Other Person's

When you speak to someone who's not interested in your story, you're discouraged from talking. On the other hand, if they nod and listen, you're happy to talk to them. And if they ask you a question on a matter that you want to talk about, you're even happier, thinking that this person is really trying to understand you.

If you nod with appropriate timing as you listen to someone speaking, and if you bring up a topic they want to talk about at just the right moment, they'll become more trusting of you. A good interviewer knows how to do this.

First, look straight into their eyes as you listen to them, and practice a nodding breath. Align your breath to their breath so that you exhale when they exhale and inhale when they inhale. If your breaths are aligned, they'll say yes to you more. One of the benefits of having a business meeting over a meal is that your breaths tend to be aligned when you're eating the same food, which makes it easier to nod and say yes.

Of course, this won't be as effective if you just do the breathing but aren't really interested. Neither is just listening enough. When they finish speaking, you need to share your ideas and opinions, asking, "Don't you think so?" or something similar so that you can lead them with your breath. This requires a great deal of study and observation of other people and their breaths. Using the technique alone won't be successful.

To practice harmonizing with other people, I'll introduce the Wave Breathing Technique

TO DISTRACT OTHERS' BREATH

A good salesperson or recruiter doesn't bring up something they want to sell right at the beginning. They know they'll be rejected, because people are always cautious with people they don't know. Rather, an expert says unimportant, undeniable things such as "Isn't it beautiful today?" so that people are left with no choice but to say yes. They may also say things to attract people's attention or interest, or compliment them to make them feel good. Once you keep saying "yes" or "I agree," it gets more difficult to say no. They can manipulate you this way. When you want to reject this, don't say "yes" too easily. Say something like "The weather is not as good as yesterday" or "It looks like it's going to rain soon," and don't say anything more.

It's important not to show your breath. In other words, keep taking long breaths and do not react to them.

SWINGING BREATHING TECHNIQUE

1. Sit on a chair and observe your natural breath. Intentionally breathe out longer before you start breathing in.

2. As you breathe out completely, you'll automatically start breathing in. Breathe in a little more intentionally.

3. Close your eyes and become aware of you body as you inhale. You may notice some contraction in your muscles or distortion in your posture that's preventing you from inhaling. Stretch those areas and correct your posture.

*Repeat steps one through three for four or five times.

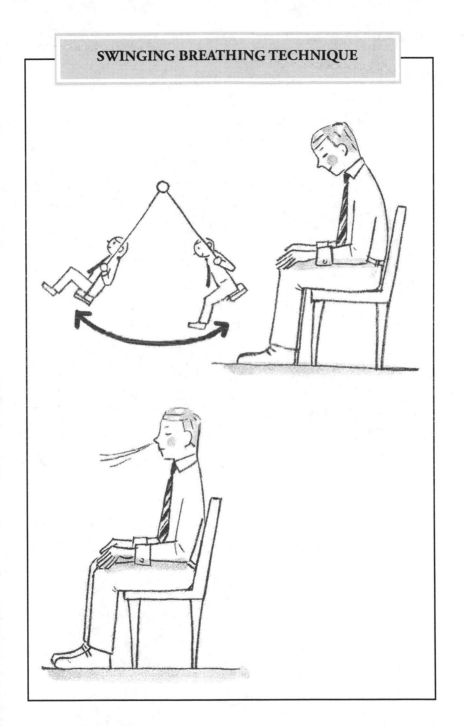

WAVE BREATHING TECHNIQUE

PRACTICING IN A PAIR (PERSON A AND B):

1. Both A and B step out with the right foot, aligning it with the other's right foot as you stand facing each other. Keep your feet wider than your hips. Bend your knees slightly and place your palms up, facing each other in front, as if holding a beach ball together.

2. Person A: Push out your hands as if pushing Person B back with the energetic ball, as you exhale. At the same time, shift your weight to your front leg and lift up your left heel. Person B: Inhale and pull back as Person A pushes you back. At the same time, shift your weight to your back leg and lift up your right toes.

3. Take turns doing these same movements. As you're being pushed, be aware of the movement of *Ki* in your partner and go with the ffow as you sense when it shifts. You can enhance your sensibility by trying to observe your partner's intention and the movement of their *Ki* without touching. Do the exercise with your left foot in front as well.

* When you practice this with a tree, do it as if you're drawing out its *Ki* as you inhale and sending out your *Ki* to the tree as you exhale.

* This is meant to be done with two persons, but you can also do it on your own using a tree.

WAVE BREATHING TECHNIQUE

22. TO RAISE A CHILD WITH A GOOD TEMPER

Even in Japan, there are many times when people get upset, lose control, and murder other people.

If parents and other adults are always angry or upset in front of children, the children learn to imitate them. Television is filled with violence and expressions that invoke emotional upheaval. There is no way that this doesn't affect our children. Everything we see, hear, or feel as we grow up registers deeply in our mind as nutrition or toxin.

Too few stimuli in today's society warm our hearts, nurture our grateful minds, or make us want to respect nature and care about every living thing. Therefore, I think it is necessary to minimize the time children spend watching TV. If it's absolutely necessary, have them watch an adorable TV show on animals, but even better, give them opportunities to play in nature.

Also, train children to be grateful during meals. I think *"Itadaki-masu"* (I respect and gratefully receive the food) before the meal and *"Gochisousamadeshita"* (thank you very much for the delicious food) after the meal are the least they can do.

It has been often shown that children today mature physically before they mature mentally because they are over-nourished. It's not unusual to find children so inflexible that they can't touch the floor when they bend forward, or have stiff shoulders or necks. They're becoming more obese too, because their parents feed them as much as they want.

I'd like to introduce the Sun Salutation Breathing Technique, which brings *Ki* down to the lower abdomen so that children will be more flexible and won't get upset as easily.

SUN SALUTATION BREATHING TECHNIQUE

1. Place your feet together and keep your palms together.

2. Breathe in and raise your hands up, looking up the sky.

3. With your palms facing front, breathe out and bring your hands down as you bend your upper body as much as possible and finish exhaling.

4. Raise your upper body as you breathe in and step out with your right foot. Finish inhaling as you bring your arms up and to your back with your chest pushed out.

5. As you exhale, bring your right foot back and your hands down to your sides and bend forward.

6. As you inhale, raise your upper body and step out with your left foot and repeat steps four and five. Then raise your upper body as you inhale, spreading your arms to the side. Bring your arms above your head and place the palms together as you finish inhaling. As you slowly breathe out, with your palms still together bring them down to your chest to finish.

23. TO EXPERIENCE DEEPER RELAXATION

Preparatory Relaxing Postures

1. Lie on your back and stretch your arms over your head with your palms together. Turn your hands out and really stretch as you make the sound "ummmmm" and stretch your Achilles tendons. Let go with a "haaaaa" sound. Repeat several times.

2. Keep your arms and legs open at about a 30-degree angle with your palms facing up, and close your eyes. Focus your mind on your breath and feel your stomach and abdomen going up and down with the breath.

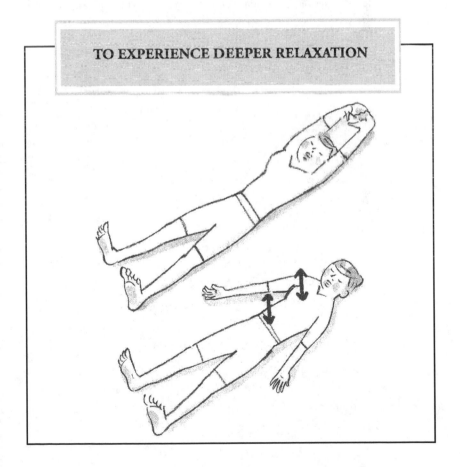

TO EXPERIENCE DEEPER RELAXATION

SELF-GUIDING RELAXATION METHOD

Progressively relax each part of your body with the natural rhythm of your breath. For each part, conduct three steps:

- guided imagination,

- confirming your guided imagination, and

- confirming your realization of the sensations from your guided imagination.

1. Bring your attention to the big toe on your right foot. Imagine that any stiffness and tension is becoming more and more relaxed as you breathe. (guided imagination)

2. On the exhalation, imagine that your toe is now loosened, relaxed, and soft (confirming your guided imagination). Even if you don't feel that way, use your imagination.

3. Confirm that you feel better—warm and good. (confirming your realization of the sensations from your guided imagination.)

Relaxation Points

Continue the exercise by focusing on the second toe of your right foot, then the third toe, and so on. Begin with the outermost parts of your body and then progress to the center. There are twenty-four relaxation points in all. Once you are used to the exercise, you can combine some points to reduce the number.

- Legs and feet—proceed from your foot to your butt in this order: each toe, bottom of the foot, top of the foot, ankle, calf, knee, thigh, butt; repeat on the other leg.

- Arms—proceed from your fingers to your shoulders in this order: each finger, palm, back of the hand, wrist, lower arm, elbow, upper arm, shoulder; repeat on the other arm.

- Upper body—proceed from your lower abdomen to your head in this order: lower abdomen, hips, upper abdomen, chest, back, throat and neck, jaw, mouth, nose, lower part of the head, eyes, ears, head, inside of the head.

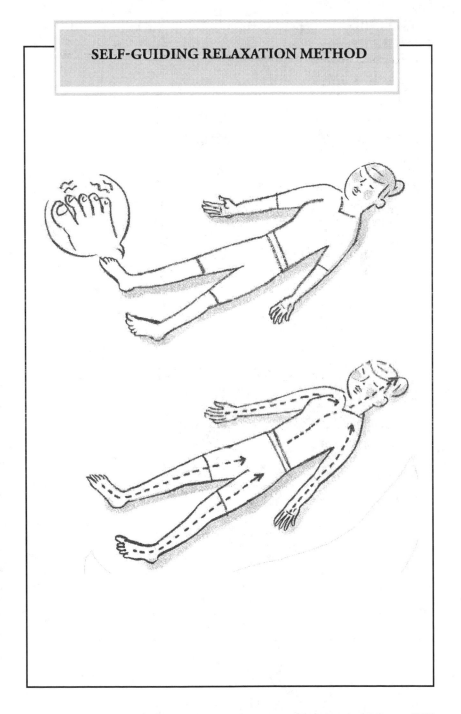

24. TO ENHANCE NATURAL HEALING ABILITY AND IMMUNITY
Preparatory Relaxing Postures
*Repeat exercise 23.

A TECHNIQUE TO INTENTIONALLY DEEPEN YOUR BREATH

1. Gradually lengthen the repeated breaths. In other words, as you breathe out naturally, tighten your abdomen slightly before the exhalation switches to inhalation, and let go of the force as you exhale intentionally.

2. As you automatically begin inhaling, breathe in naturally. Expand your stomach slightly before the inhalation switches to exhalation, and let go of the force as you breathe in intentionally.

3. As you automatically begin exhaling, breathe out naturally. Then, as you did in step one, tighten your abdomen slightly and breathe out intentionally before the exhalation switches to inhalation, then breathe in as you did in step one.

* Repeat steps one and two several times, enlarging each time as if swinging on a swing.

* Do the Swinging Breathing Technique on your back, breathing through your nose.

KI ENERGY CHARGING BREATHING TECHNIQUE

1. Imagine that your natural breath has become bigger, and intentionally increase the density of *Ki* energy. When you inhale, imagine that all the *Ki* entrances of your body are wide open and that lively energy is coming in and being stored in your *Tanden*. Breathe in so that your lower stomach expands.

2. When your breath is at 80 percent capacity, hold it without straining. Push the air into your stomach so that it can't leak out, and tighten your anus. Imagine that there is an energetic ball in your *Tanden* that is holding the absorbed *Ki* and being charged with it, becoming more powerful. Your stomach should feel like a plastic ball as you hold your breath.

3. Start exhaling slowly, imagining that the leftover air is leaving your body as you tighten your stomach. Exhale intentionally and completely. Take a natural breath, and go back to step one.

25. RELAXED STANDING

In Asia, there is a traditional type of meditation that is practiced on the feet. When you're standing, you can't be stable if your body is distorted because it causes strains and pains in your body. In addition, if your internal organs are too low or if you have a weak back and abdominal muscles, you may feel tired or sick. If you feel tired, make sure that your spine is not distorted, but naturally curved, and that your back and abdominal muscles are strong and flexible so that your body is straight even when affected by gravity. You need to be able to do deep abdominal breathing to help your blood circulate against gravity. Start practicing for a short period, like five minutes, then correct yourself on both the physical and *Ki* levels so that you can gradually stand for a longer time.

Let's practice standing in alignment with gravity. Keep your feet together with your big toes touching. Beginners can keep their legs hip-width apart to make it easier. Hang your arms naturally by your side and straighten your upper body. Don't push out your chin or chest. Close your eyes gently, and carefully look for a position that suits you as you stand perpendicular to gravity like an egg standing on end. Gradually correct your posture by breathing naturally. Try to let go of any unnecessary strain as you find the right position. Keep breathing naturally as you melt into the balance of the centripetal force (gravity) and centrifugal force of the earth.

Here's how to relax in a standing position.

Keep your feet hip-width apart. Keep your fifth toes parallel and your knees slightly bent. Hang your arms naturally at your side and close your eyes gently. Separate your body into five sections: right, left, front, back, and center. Through self-guided relaxation, begin relaxing each section, starting at the top of your head and moving to the lower areas. Guide yourself with three steps: (1) guided imagination that you are becoming loose and relaxed, (2) confirming your guided imagination that you are now loose and relaxed, and (3) confirming your realization of the sensations from the guided imagination that you feel good and relaxed.

Order of Relaxation

- Right side—proceed in the following order: right side of the head and neck, right shoulder, right arm, right hand, right side of the torso, right hip, outside of the right leg, side of the right foot.

- Left side—proceed in the following order: left side of the head and neck, left shoulder, left arm, left hand, left side of the torso, outside of the left leg, side of the left foot.

- Front—proceed in the following order: front of the head, face, neck, chest, upper and lower abdomen, legs, top of the feet.

- Back—proceed in the following order: back of the head and neck, back, hips, butt, back of the legs, bottom of the feet.

- Inner—proceed in the following order: inside of the head and neck, inside of the chest, inside of the upper and lower stomach, inside and inner part of the legs.

*Practice standing perpendicular to gravity by keeping your feet together with your big toes touching.

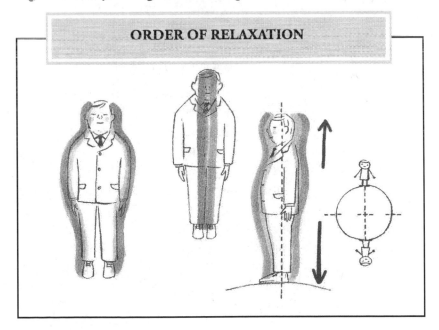

ORDER OF RELAXATION

Conclusion:
Turning Daily Activities into Training

I practice breathing techniques when I walk to the station or climb the stairs at the station. My mind is always focused on my posture, movement, and breath so that I can learn such things as how to breathe in order to avoid getting tired when carrying heavy luggage.

People often ask me why I always walk with heavy luggage. It's so that I can use my daily activities to train as much as possible, because I don't have enough time to exercise my muscles. Even when I climb a high mountain like Mt. Fuji, I never get a headache or other ailments like many people do, because I take each step with good breath. I don't necessarily climb fast like some people, because keeping my own pace is an important aspect of my breathing practice. Whenever I get injured, by falling for example, I study how to ease the pain through breathing techniques, because it's such a wasted opportunity if I just let it be and have the injury treated by other people.

People I've taught often tell me that practicing the Breathing Exercise or Cleansing Breathing Technique successfully helped them prevent a hangover or ease a toothache. In many cases, someone who used to get tired just going grocery shopping is no longer tired, or someone who could never travel due to motion sickness now travels all over the world with me to teach yoga and breathing techniques. Most of these people look very thin and weak, but they are surprisingly capable of surviving tight schedules when we work together.

These results of greater endurance and stronger muscles are not acquired through physical training. I think it's because, through this practice, people learn to breathe more deeply, even when they're not consciously doing so, which enables them to be more relaxed and manage difficult situations. I believe that anyone can activate their hidden ability by practicing breathing techniques. So let's just do it.

Last but not least, I'd like to give my deepest gratitude and thanks to Yumi Yamaoka, who gave me the opportunity to write this book; Setsuko Kaga, who helped edit it; Mle Kadokuchi, who draw the nice illustrations; Makoto Fujimura, who designed it; Dr. Masaji Nisimoto, whose scientific point of view I consulted; and Atsuko Masuda of Soushi-sha.

Osamu Tatsumura
Gassho, *August 2002*

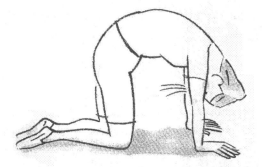

Healing Yoga
for Beginners

EASY YOGA BREATHING EXERCISE 1
Basic abdominal breathing (to exhale all out)

Effect

Abdominal breathing is called so because the abdomen moves along with the breath which is unlike thoracic breathing. Actually, it is a breathing technique which tenses and relaxes diaphragms above dome-like lower ribcage, in other words, it is a breathing technique which lowers the air pressure in thorax with up and down motion and takes in the outside air into the lungs. It can take in more air than inhaling the air with up-down and open-close motion of ribcages. Not only it's beneficial because of more oxygen inhaled, it also betters the blood circulation of intestines because it massages the lower abdomen. It also makes it easier to gather more power in the abdominal area, so you can maintain natural state of body, which is empty in the upper body and filled in the lower body.

Order of movements, breathing, and focus of mind

1. Sit in the chair or on the ffoor, with your back muscles straight and your shoulders and neck relaxed. Place your hands on your thighs with the palms facing up. When seen from the front, your nose, the center of chest, and navel have to be aligned, and when seen from the side, your ear, tip of your shoulder, and the base of pelvis have to be aligned.

2. Push your abdomen in as you breathe out, and exhale out all the air. Try to focus on just exhaling everything in this.

3. Inhale as much as you can, and be aware that you are naturally inhaling without effort as you relax the force that was tightening your abdomen.

4. Your exhale should be twice as long as your inhale. Do it 10 times as a set and do 2 sets a day.
   * Start with an easier length such as exhaling in 8 counts and inhaling in 4 counts.

EASY YOGA BREATHING EXERCISE 2
Basic thoracic breathing (to expand sideways)

Effect

Thoracic breathing is called so because it moves the chest which is unlike abdominal breathing exercise. Actually, it is a technique to lower the air pressure in thorax and take in the air into the lungs by opening and closing the ribs. When opening and closing the ribs, the chest moves to 3 different directions; up and down, left and right, and back and forth. It seems like most people consider only the upward motion amoloorng all as thoracic breathing. However, sideway motion allows more air in among all three. Thoracic breathing in Yoga is not what the general public thinks thoracic breathing is. By following the instruction below to expand vertically, horizontally, and front and back, you can inhale almost as much of air as you can with abdominal breathing.

Order of movements, breathing, and focus of mind

1. Sit in the chair or on the floor, with your back muscles straight and shoulders and neck relaxed. Place your hands on your thighs with the palms facing up. When seen from the front, your nose, the center of chest, and navel have to be aligned, and when seen from the side, your ear, tip of your shoulder, and the base of pelvis have to be aligned.

2. Push your abdomen in as you breathe out, and exhale out all the air. Try to focus on just exhaling everything in this.

3. With your abdomen still tightened, inhale by expanding ribs to the side with intention to expand them front and back too. Then breathe in to the limit as if you are pulling up your chest.

4. Once it's filled up, exhale as you relax your chest.

5. Repeat 2 through 4.

EASY YOGA BREATHING EXERCISE 3
Basic thoracic and abdominal alternating breathing practice

Effect
In the natural state, human breath consists of both thoracic and abdominal but it's more likely to be abdominal in a calm state. However, when trying to inhale, most people tend to inhale with thoracic breathing by pulling up the chest unintentionally. Therefore don't get tense when you try to inhale and try to do abdominal breathing, and then thoracic one after another. By being aware of the difference, you can eliminate the habitual link between inhaling and tension of sympathetic nerves, and you can practice the technique to deepen your breath.

Order of movements, breathing, and focus of mind

1. Sit in the chair or on the floor, with your back muscles straight and shoulders and neck relaxed. Place your hands on your thighs with the palms facing up. When seen from the front, your nose, the center of chest, and navel have to be aligned, and when seen from the side, your ear, tip of your shoulder, and the base of pelvis have to be aligned.

2. Push in the abdomen as you exhale and relax when you exhale about 80% of the air, and inhale with abdominal breathing to fill up 80%, and exhale what you inhaled.

3. Maintain the force to tighten the abdomen, then open your chest to breathe in. When you inhale to fill about 80%, relax and exhale what you inhaled.

4. Again, relax your abdomen to inhale and exhale the same way. Repeat abdominal and thoracic breathing alternately for 10 times.

EASY YOGA BREATHING EXERCISE 4
Basic kapalabhati breathing technique to quickly exhale and slowly inhale.
It's significance is kapala (skull) and bhati (light).

Effect
Breathing techniques vary from just inhaling and exhaling of air to applying ki or prana, but here I'd like to discuss in a basic level.

Exercised muscles can contract fast but loose or tight muscles cannot contract quickly. The respiratory muscles get loose or stiff as well. If you continue breathing shallowly the movement becomes dull and it contracts and expands more slowly. Traditional kapalabhati breathing technique is to exhale intentionally moving the respiratory muscles (such as diaphragms) quickly and to inhale letting the muscles go back to the way it was. You need to breathe normally and calmly for at least 1 minute.

Order of movements, breathing, and focus of mind

1. Sit in the chair or on the floor, with your back muscles straight and shoulders and neck relaxed. Place your hands on your thighs with the palms facing up. When seen from the front, your nose, the center of chest, and navel have to be aligned, and when seen from the side, your ear, tip of your shoulder, and the base of pelvis have to be aligned.

2. Close your mouth tightly and touch the roof of the mouth with tip of tongue, eliminate the air in the mouth, and inhale.

3. Then quickly exhale through the nose with "hmmm" sound and contract the abdomen, and then relax the abdomen to naturally inhale through the nose. Inhale about 80% and exhale quickly again. Repeat the breath 10 times and start breathing naturally.

* Stop immediately if you start feeling dizzy.

EASY YOGA BREATHING EXERCISE 5
Introduction to basic fast breathing technique bhastrika

Effect

Bhastrika is bellows which is used to send some air into the fire to make it bigger. This breathing technique is to send prana or ki to the body in the same manner. It is based on the idea that we should bring in lots of air to make the fire bigger. It is a technique to quickly take in prana into the body, activate, and energize. It quickly stretches respiratory muscles such as the abdominal muscles to strengthen them well, and it helps the blood circulation in the internal organs, and your breath will be deeper even when you are not conscious of it.

In the beginning start with 20 times in a short period of time, with the pace of twice in a second and then increase it to three times gradually. Breathe naturally for a minute after the practice.

Order of movements, breathing, and focus of mind

1. Sit in the chair or on the floor, with your back muscles straight and shoulders and neck relaxed. Place your hands on your thighs with the palms facing up. When seen from the front, your nose, the center of chest, and navel have to be aligned, and when seen from the side, your ear, tip of your shoulder, and the base of pelvis have to be aligned.

2. Close your mouth tightly and touch the roof of the mouth with the tip of your tongue and eliminate the air in the mouth.

3. Exhale quickly through your nose with "hmmm" sound and tighten your abdomen, and then inhale fast and rhythmically. The ratio of the length of the breath should be 1:1. Your abdomen would move like that of a snake. Keep your chest still. If you feel sick, stop immediately.

EASY YOGA BREATHING EXERCISE 6
Intentional abdominal double breathing technique

Effect

We previously learned how to breathe quickly. This time we practice to breathe consciously controlling the length of inhalation and exhalation. From the time of Buddha, it has been taught that we need to exhale twice as long as inhaling. The difference of inffuence that inhalation and exhalation would have on us on autonomic nerve level is that inhalation stimulates sympathetic nerves and exhalation stimulates parasympathetic nerves. If you want to be agitated or excited inhale fast and strong and if you want to calm down exhale slow and long. If you inhale long with your eyes closed, your brain wave would be more likely to be ffistate.

Order of movements, breathing, and focus of mind

1. Sit in the chair or on the ffoor, with your back muscles straight and shoulders and neck relaxed. Place your hands on your thighs with the palms facing up. When seen from the front, your nose, the center of chest, and navel have to be aligned, and when seen from the side, your ear, tip of your shoulder, and the base of pelvis have to be aligned. Close your mouth tightly and touch the roof of the mouth with tip of tongue, eliminate the air in the mouth, and inhale.

2. Exhale slowly with your eyes closed. Using your abdominal muscles push in and tighten your abdomen and also tighten your anus.

3. Once you finish exhaling, relax your body and let it naturally inhale.

4. When natural inhalation stops, exhale again intentionally.

* Exhalation should be twice as long as the length of inhalation. If you inhale in 6 counts, exhale in 12 counts. If you do this more than 5 minutes, you would be more likely to be in α state.

EASY YOGA BREATHING EXERCISE 7
Basic One nostril breathing technique

Effect

Here we'll try the technique to breathe through one nostril at a time. Our nostrils are usually not equally clear, and one is usually better than the other. In yoga, it is believed that the yin and yang balance of ki is good when both nostrils are equally clear. If you practice to thoroughly breathe through each nostril, your awareness on breath will be stronger and autonomic nerves will be balanced better.

Order of movements, breathing, and focus of mind

1. Sit in the chair or on the floor, with your back muscles straight and shoulders and neck relaxed. Place your hands on your thighs with the palms facing up. When seen from the front, your nose, the center of chest, and navel have to be aligned, and when seen from the side, your ear, tip of your shoulder, and the base of pelvis have to be aligned. Close your mouth tightly and touch the roof of the mouth with tip of tongue, eliminate the air in the mouth, and inhale.

2. Then, close the right nostril with right thumb and keep the right index and middle fingers in between the eyebrows. Keep the left nostril open and lightly touch the the wing of the nose with right ring finger.

3. First, inhale thoroughly through the left nostril in about 8 counts, and when it's filled about 80% close the left nostril with right ring finger as well.

4. Then let the right nostril open and exhale in about 8 counts.

5. Once you exhale all out, thoroughly inhale through right nostril in about 8 counts.

6. After 9 counts close the right nostril and open left nostril to inhale in 8 counts.

* Repeat the both sides about 10 times.

EASY YOGA BREATHING EXERCISE 8
Applied one nostril breathing technique 1

Effect

Here we practice one nostril breathing again but this time we ffow ki energy while we breathe using visualization. The breathing exercises in yoga are less effective if consciousness and breath are not aligned. It enhances the balance of autonomic nerves and energy in the air is more absorbed, and alters the senses of the skin which as a result beautifies the skin.

Order of movements, breathing, and focus of mind

1. Sit in the chair or on the ffoor, with your back muscles straight and shoulders and neck relaxed. Place your hands on your thighs with the palms facing up. When seen from the front, your nose, the center of chest, and navel have to be aligned, and when seen from the side, your ear, tip of your shoulder, and the base of pelvis have to be aligned. Close your mouth tightly and touch the roof of the mouth with tip of tongue, eliminate the air in the mouth, and inhale.

2. Then, close the right nostril with right thumb and keep the right index and middle fingers in between the eyebrows. Keep the left nostril open and lightly touch the wing of the nose with right ring finger.

3. Inhale thoroughly through the left nostril in more than 8 counts. While inhaling, imagine your left body is beamed with light and breathe as if you are absorbing the light. When you inhaled about 80%, close the left nostril with the right ring finger. (Visualize your left body becoming brighter)

4. Open the right nostril and exhale in more than 8 counts.

5. Once you exhaled it all out, inhale thoroughly through right nostril in more than 8 counts, as if you are absorbing the light that's shining upon your right body. Visualize your right body becoming brighter.

6. When you inhaled about 80%, close the right nostril, open the left one, and exhale in 8 counts.

* Repeat this 10 times on each side.

* As each side gets brighter each time, imagine the entire body gradually becomes illuminating.

EASY YOGA BREATHING EXERCISE 9
Applied one nostril breathing 2

Effect

Here we practice to breathe with one nostril again, but this time we learn to purify the path of ki by changing the speed of breath. The air travels through the paths faster, cleansing the paths quickly, so that ki can be absorbed fresh. It also corrects the unbalanced clearness of both nostrils quickly. It also strengthens the respiratory ability because the respiratory muscles are quickly stretched.

Order of movements, breathing, and focus of mind

1. Sit in the chair or on the ffoor, with your back muscles straight and shoulders and neck relaxed. Place your hands on your thighs with the palms facing up. When seen from the front, your nose, the center of chest, and navel have to be aligned, and when seen from the side, your ear, tip of your shoulder, and the base of pelvis have to be aligned. Close your mouth tightly and touch the roof of the mouth with tip of tongue, eliminate the air in the mouth, and inhale.

2. Then, close the right nostril with right thumb and keep the right index and middle fingers in between the eyebrows. Keep the left nostril open and lightly touch the wing of the nose with right ring finger.

3. Quickly inhale through the left nostril in half a second, and quickly close the left nostril, and open the right nostril at the same time and exhale through it in half a second.

4. Then quickly inhale through the right nostril in half a second, and close it, and open and exhale through the left one in half a second.

* Count each breath up to 30 times in the beginning. When you are done 30 times, breathe normally, trying to observe the change in the inner nostrils, and start again.

EASY YOGA BREATHING EXERCISE 10
Aoum mantra breathing technique (meditation)

Effect

In ancient India, sounds and words were said to have power, and certain sounds were supposed represent god. Among these, three sounds of A O UM are considered to be special and holy, and it is said that you can harmonize with the universe by vocalizing the sound. Its significance is different from what is know to Japanese as AOUM breathing. Tests of brain wave have shown that anyone can easily get into α state, *gyan mudra* by vocalizing these sounds. If you practice this a few times before a meal, you can calm down and prevent overeating.

Order of movements, breathing, and focus of mind

1. Sit on a chair with your back straight and neck and shoulders relaxed. Place your hands on your thighs where it's easy for your breath with palms facing up, and make a wing of the nose with your thumb and index finger creating a circle and rest of the fingers straight. In the correct sitting position, exhale all the air out, and slightly arch your back, and inhale fully. Your eyes are half open.

2. When you finish inhaling, keeping the posture, exhale with sounds "Ahhhh" "Ohhhh" and "Ummmm" in one breath. The key is to vocalize them from the bottom of your abdomen as if it's ringing throughout your body. You vocalize the sound that make you feel the best longer than the rest. As you practice this, move shift your posture; at "Ah" sound, your back is arched, at "Oh" sound, it's slightly tilted forward, and at "Um" sound, finish exhaling and bring the body back to the center.

3. When you complete exhaling and your body is back at the center, inhale and repeat. You should repeat this at least 7 times.

EASY YOGA BREATHING EXERCISE 11
Stabilizing breathing technique

Effect

When you want to stabilize your mind, you cannot just give it an order. Therefore, you need to intentionally create a state of body and breath which makes it easy to calm the mind. This technique is to control the mind using the breath and the body. Slow breath and repeated movement of stretching the back to exhale really helps to calm your mind quickly. By touching the ffoor with your forehead, you can cultivate more grateful and humbled mind for the earth and also the force that sustains all living things.

Order of movements, breathing, and focus of mind

1. Sit in the *seiza* position with your back straight and neck and shoulders relaxed. Open your arms to the side at the height of the shoulders, and bend the elbows o create L form. Make a light fist with your thumb folded in. Then exhale out completely.

2. Inhale as you tilt your upper body backward.

3. Then exhale as you bring your upper body forward, and touch the ffoor with your forehead. Stretch your arms in front and tighten your abdomen as you exhale completely.

4. Then bring the body back up as you inhale, and arch back to go back to the position in step 2 and finish inhaling. Repeat this several times.

EASY YOGA BREATHING EXERCISE 12
Lion breathing technique

Effect

When you want to be active and energetic, it would be difficult if your breath was weak. This lion breathing technique is to intentionally create a state of body and breath to make you more active. It was inspired by a lion which roars so powerfully. Its uniqueness lies in how you open our chest to breathe in and stick out your tongue, and then push out your chest and stretch your back as you push your knees with your hands to breathe out strongly with fore in your lower back. This breath and posture would be helpful to quickly and strongly activate your mind.

Order of movements, breathing, and focus of mind

1. Sit on the ffoor with your knees wide apart and with your toes standing on the ffoor. Keep your back straight and relax your neck and shoulders. Place your hands on your knees with Place your hands on your knees, as if your nails were clawing into the knees, then exhale completely.

2. Then inhale fully as you push down your knees and pus out your chest.

3. Then exhale strongly with "haaaa" sound sticking out your tongue. As you do this, tighten your pelvis, stretch your spine, keep your eyes wide open, and keep exhaling as much as you can as if you are a lion roaring.

4. When you finish exhaling, relax your body, inhale slowly, and get back to the original state. Repeat it several times.

EASY YOGA BREATHING EXERCISE 13
Inhalation 1: exhalation 2 breathing technique

Effect

Since the time of Buddha (about 2500 years ago) the connection between the state of mind and breath has been well understood. The influence the inhalation and exhalation have over our body and mind are opposite. Breath with more emphasis on inhalation leads to tension and slow exhalation leads to peace of mind. If you want to calm your mind, breathe out more than twice as long as breathing in. Also, rhythmically repeated breath for a certain period of time creates a relaxing state for body and mind. This time, you breathe out twice as long as you breathe in, and repeat this rhythmically for more than 10 times. If you tighten your abdominal muscles and strengthen your tanden as you exhale, a hormone called serotonin is released in your brain and it prepares the body and mind for activity.

Order of movements, breathing, and focus of mind

1. Sit on a chair or sit in seiza position, keeping your spine straight, with your hands on your legs wherever it's comfortable with the palms facing up. Exhale completely.

2. Then inhale through your nose evenly and steadily, for 4 counts for example. Do not try to inhale so much and fill about 80%.

3. Then exhale twice as long as inhaling, in 8 counts in this case. Intentionally tighten your abdomen when you exhale. * Keep the same rhythm and intentionally repeat this process for more than 10 minutes.

4. Once you are finished, breathe naturally and observe the changes of mind and body.

EASY YOGA BREATHING EXERCISE 14
Inhalation 4: holding 7: exhalation 8 breathing technique

Effect

Dr. Andrew Weil, one of the most acknowledged holistic healers in US, introduces this breathing technique of inhaling in 4 counts, holding in 7 counts, and exhaling in 8 counts as "relaxing breathing exercise" or natural sedative. You inhale through your nose and exhale through your mouth with "shhhhh" sound. Exhaling through your mouth with the sound helps to purify *jaki* or bad energy, and holding the breath helps to absorb more *ki* or energy.

Order of movements, breathing, and focus of mind

1. Sit on a chair or sit in *seiza* position, keeping your spine straight, with your hands on your legs wherever it's comfortable with the palms facing up. Exhale completely.

2. Then breathe in through your nose in 4 counts evenly. Do not try to inhale so much and fill about 80%.

3. Then hold the breath for 7 counts. While doing this you can absorb *ki* or energy from the air you have taken in.

4. Then exhale through your mouth with "shhhh" sound in 8 counts. As you do so, intentionally squeeze your abdomen.

5. With the same rhythm, do 4 cycles at a time, twice a day.

6. When you are done, breathe naturally for several minutes, and observe changes of your mind or body.

* Even if 1 count is 1 second, it only takes 19 seconds to do it, so anyone can do it.

EASY YOGA BREATHING EXERCISE 15
Navel breathing technique

Effect

Navel was an entry way of all the energies including blood stream when we were in the mother's womb. This function stopped upon our birth and our nose and mouth became the entry way for the basic energies. However, in ancient India, it was thought that the navel is one of the entrances for the unseen energy, and breathing through the navel was supposed to bring in the energy for the mind and spirit. Of course you are not going to breathe the air through your navel, but it helps you to focus your attention on your navel, and you will be guided to deeper abdominal breathing and relaxation.

It will fill you with sense of oneness with the universe and sense of peace like being held by your mother.

Order of movements, breathing, and focus of mind

1. Lie on your back and keep your hands on your abdomen, creating a triangle with your index fingers and thumbs touching lightly. Keep your navel at the center of the triangle.

2. Then focus your awareness on the navel and imagine as if it is connected to the universe through an invisible pipe of light, and feel that your abdomen gets bigger and smaller as you breathe.

3. When you inhale, imagine prana (ki or universal energy) enters the body through the navel and spreads throughout the body, energizing each cell of the body.

4. When you exhale, imagine the air whose nutrition has all been absorbed leaving the body empty.

5. Repeat this about 10 times slowly without any strains and breathe naturally.

EASY YOGA BREATHING EXERCISE 16
Ujjayi breathing (practiced on the chair)

Effect

In Japan, we categorize the breathing into groups based on the body part that we use such as abdominal or thoracic breath, but in pranayama in Indian tradition such classification is considered to take away the important essence of breathing. Ujjayi breathing is inspired from an image that a victorious man breathing proudly with his chest wide open. It is not a typical thoracic breathing; it is unique because you are supposed to open your chest wide to the side.

You breathe slowly opening your chest, so it expands the thoracic cages and it is effective to balance the blood pressure or calm down the nerves.

Order of movements, breathing, and focus of mind

1. Keep your spine straight and sit in a yogic posture or on a chair with your knees appropriately apart. Make circles with your thumbs and index fingers and keep them on your thighs. Pull your chin in so it touches the upper part of your chest and close your eyes and focus you awareness on the inside of your lungs.

2. Inhale slowly through the nostrils. Try to fill up the lungs by breathing at the same speed and same amount steadily. Slightly tighten your throat, making the "shhh" sound in your throat, and expand the chest sideways. Breathe in as much as you can without expanding your abdomen.

3. When you exhale, try to breathe out with "haaa" sound at the same speed ad amount of air as inhaling. When you exhale try to feel the air at the back of the roof of your mouth. Pause for a while before you inhale or exhale. Do this at least 10 times.

EASY YOGA BREATHING EXERCISE 17
Regular silence abdominal breathing technique

Effect

When we try to concentrate, we naturally stop breathing or breathe more gently and silently. In order to control the state of mind with breath, you need to closely relate your awareness to the respiratory muscles, and try to breathe steadily. The exercise to breathe at the same speed letting in and out the same amount of air is helpful to intentionally control the respiratory system. If you control the entrance and exit of the breath with your lower abdomen (tanden), you can concentrate for a long time without being nervous.

Order of movements, breathing, and focus of mind

1. With your spine straight, sit in a yogic posture or on a chair with he knees moderately wide apart. Make circles with your index fingers and thumbs on your thighs. Keep your neck straight, close your eyes, and focus your attention to lower abdomen or tanden.

2. Slowly exhale through your nostrils. Try to keep the same speed and pace the same amount of air, and slowly tighten your lower abdomen. Be aware it gradually gets pushed it. Do this without making noise, gently.

3. Gently inhale at the same speed allowing the same amount of air flow in constantly, and be aware that your lower abdomen expands. Try to breathe as long as you can but not to an extent to suffer or loose control of the pace. Try to exhale longer than inhaling. Do this like a wave that comes and goes.

EASY YOGA BREATHING EXERCISE 18
Feet breathing technique lying on the floor

Effect

When we try to concentrate our mind, it is easier if we pay attention to our breath and concentrate on it. As you do this, instead of paying attention to your upper body, pay attention to the lower abdomen or feet so that you can cultivate more natural way of being which is empty in the upper body and full in the lower body. In this breathing technique, the air would actually comes in through your nose, but by focusing your awareness to the bottom of the feet as you continue breathing, ki flows better from the feet to tanden and fills tanden, calming the mind and ki and making it easier to control them.

Order of movements, breathing, and focus of mind

1. Lie on your back and keep your feet hip width apart. Create circles with thumbs and index fingers and keep them on the ffoor slightly off of the body. Close your eyes lightly and focus your awareness on your feet.

2. Breathe slowly through the nose, focusing on the toes. Imagine ki ffows in through the toes as you breathe in, traveling up the legs, lower abdomen, and to tanden, filling and energizing the area.

3. When it's 80% full, hold the breath and imagine your tanden being charged and the ki energy travels throughout the body.

4. When you exhale, stretch your Achilles tendons, and imagine the left-over air and residue travels from tanden downwards and leaves from the bottom of the feet.

5. Inhaling: holding: exhaling should be 1:1:2 ratio, and start with 4 counts as 1 or so. Do about 10 cycles.

EASY YOGA BREATHING EXERCISE 19
Elimination breathing technique

Effect

Breathing techniques that accompany expansion and contraction of abdomen in general helps to enhance the elimination ability. Here I'd like to introduce what you can practice while you are sitting on a toilet. It activates the bowel movement by rhythmically tightening the abdomen with abdominal breath and twisting the upper body left and right at the same time. If you are constipated please try it.

Order of movements, breathing, and focus of mind

1. Sit on a toilet or a chair of the same height to practice. Keep the knees apart, place the hands on the knees, slightly stick out the butt, and keep the abdomen and back straight.

2. Exhale out through your nose and tighten the abdomen. Slightly twist the upper body to the left and right and slide your upper body. Come back to the center as you breathe in. The key is to do it rhythmically.

*When you slide to the left, push the right knee with the right hand and exhale as you slightly twist to the left. Slide in about 3 counts and inhale in 1 to 2 counts and get back to the center, and do the other side.

EASY YOGA BREATHING EXERCISE 20
Ki energy charging breathing technique

Effect

Breathe with appropriate ratio of inhaling, holding, and exhaling of breath, and try to absorb as much energy from the air as you are holding it. Its relaxing effect will be greater than just lying on the ffoor and breathe.

Order of movements, breathing, and focus of mind

1. Lie on the ffoor with the legs apart in about 30 degrees. Arms are also 30 degrees apart from the body with the palms facing up. Keep a relaxing posture and let go of your body.

2. Slowly breathe in through your nose with your eyes closed and imagine you are absorbing the energy into your abdomen. Keep imagining that this life force energy is ffowing to you more and more and your body is becoming more energized.

3. When you fill yourself up, hold the breath as much as you are comfortable. Then visualize you are taking in as much of prana or ki and oxygen fom the air that you are holding in your lungs.

4. exhale "paaaaa" and breathe naturally several times to rest, and get back to the step 2 to repeat.

* If you do this well, you will feel very good.

Breathe is life, and breathing is to live.

About the Author & Translator

OSAMU TATSUMURA is the director of Tatsumura Yoga Research Institute. He is the founder of International Holistic Life Yoga Study Association, and president of Oki Yoga Association

He was born in Hyogo, Japan, in 1948, and he graduated from Waseda University, with BA in literature. In 1973, he began his training with Master Masahiro Oki, the pioneer of holistic yoga and the holistic way of healing, eating, and thinking in Japan who revolutionized the concept of yoga and created Oki Yoga. Oki Yoga is based on Zen Buddhism, Shinto practice, Chinese Do-In, Qi Gong, and the original essence of Indian yoga. Since then, Master Tatsumura has been working all over the world as the leader of Oki Yoga.

After the passing of Master Oki in 1985, he became the head of the Oki Yoga Institute. In 1994, he founded the Tatsumura Yoga Research Institute. He also founded Space Gaia, where he has been training future holistic health leaders. He encourages people to create body, mind, and spirit with oriental wisdom, so that we can all listen to the words of Mother Earth and the Life Force Energy given to us from the Universe. He has written numerous articles and books, and travels all over the world teaching and giving lectures.

KAZUKO TATSUMURA HILLYER, OMD, PhD, graduated from Toho Academy of Music, Boston University, New York University, and the International Academy of Education. She currently serves as director of *Gaia Holistic Health Center* and *Okido Holistic Ltd.* in New York, as well as directing the *World Women Peace Foundation* and *World Religion Federation*. Dr. Hillyer's numerous achievements and awards in the field of the arts, humanitarian work include: The Distinguished Service Medal for contribution of culture and society by the Foundation of Japan Culture Promotion; the Smetana Medal (Czechoslovakia); the Gold Medal of Cultural Merit (Austria); and recognition for "Specially Distinguished Services" (France), and holistic health include the National Congressional Committee's 2003 Physician of the Year award. An internationally respected healer and educator, she lectures on health and spirituality and conducts seminars on a variety of topics around the world.